School Based Assessment

School Based Assessment

Theory into Practice

Dr. Pritam Singh

SP SHIPRA
SHIPRA

ISBN: 978-81-7541-572-0

First Published in India in 2011

School Based Assessment: Theory into Practice

Published by:
SHIPRA PUBLICATIONS
H.O.: LG 18-19, Pankaj Central Market, I.P. Ext.,
Patparganj, Delhi-110092, Tel: 91-11-22236152, 22235152
Br.Off. 4617/18, Ansari Road, Darya Ganj,
New Delhi-110002, Tel: 65946453
E-mail: info@shiprapublications.com
www.shiprapublications.com

Contents

Preface

In view of emerging societal needs and corresponding changes occurring in the educational system, pattern of assessment and evaluation system has also to be reviewed to meet those demands. The first chapter of the book provides historical retrospect reflecting the changing emphases in reforming the assessment system in our schools. It was also considered necessary for practicing teachers to understand the proper use of the emerged web of technical terms which are defined and grouped in tripartite classification in the next chapter. Trend towards de-emphasising the eternal examinations and increasing concern for school based assessment system of continuous and comprehensive evaluation necessitates to high light the philosophy underlying school based assessment to enable the teachers to appreciate the fundamental basis on which assessment objectives are formulated in terms of intended learning outcomes, as described in separate chapters. To make assessment system publically acceptable, and functionally operative the underlying key concepts for developing assessment objectives are explained in a separate chapter. International scenario is depicted in a separate chapter to describe the emergent trends in terms of internal and external assessment. It is followed by a chapter on development of conceptual map reflecting paradigm, components and modes of assessment and management issues.

Based on conceptual map, a growth oriented model of assessment is suggested in a separate chapter, that is theoretically tenable, pedagogically sound and administratively feasible, However to put this model into practice functional operationally strategy has to be adopted using participatory approach with planned introduction, proper monitoring and evaluation as described in chapter 9.

How to promote quality of education through assessment specific measures are suggested like stating success indicators, sustainable strategy of implementation and using assessment for improving teaching learning process as indicated in chapter 10. Since impact of assessment is conditioned by the learning environments of the institution undertaking annual school self-evaluation is essential to judge adequacies and inadequacies of processes and products of performance on the basis of which steps can be taken to improve teaching, learning and assessment practices as discussed in chapter 11.

In the next chapter role of research and other support services in highlighted to enable the teachers to make use of research based outcomes to improve the existing practices in teaching, learning and testing. In spite of all efforts made from time to time at various levels we have failed to make internal assessment a functional alternative to external mode of examination system. Where do we fail, is analysed in the next chapter, along with practical measures. In the last chapter crucial emerging issues are deliberated upon to draw attention of the practioners as to how best they can make school based assessment administratively functional, participatory, pedagogically sound and cost effective. For successful implementation of the proposed model of school based assessment we have to develop complete faith in teachers' competency as well as their right to assess their wards who alone can make the school based assessment continuous, comprehensive and competency based in practice if administrative support of training and retraining of staff is provided besides ensuring research and other support services.

On the basis of my experience in the field of testing, evaluation and examination reform for three decades at state, national and international level I do hope that for improving school based assessment practices, this book would appeal as a practical guide to inservice teachers, teacher educators of training colleges, S.C.E.R.Ts, D.I.E.T.s, school administrators and supervisors, school counsellors and researchers who are concerned with improving the existing practices in school based assessment and learning environments of the institutions and even all stake holders who are interested in making school based assessment publically acceptable, democratic, comprehensive, trustworthy and functionally operative.

I take this opportunity to acknowledge my grateful thanks to Dr. A.K. Sharma, former Director NCERT, Dr.Ved Prakash Vice Chairman U.G.C and Dr. R.N. Mehrotra former Head Department of Education, Delhi University with whom I discussed and finalized the chapterisation of this book before writing the text. I am specially obliged to the great educationist Dr. Amrik Singh for providing me the needed guidance from time to time to finalise he text material. I am thankful to all those authors whose books I consulted and got useful ideas for inclusion in my book. Lastly, I am thankful to Shipra Publications who gladly accepted to publish the book.

Dr. Pritam Singh

1

Historical Perspective of Internal Assessment

1.1 Assessment Practices upto the 20th Century

Before taking up the various practices let us first realize how examinations have played influential role in human history. Examinations, which originated in antiquity, have been considered as judgmental devices, a sacred cow, a Socratic quiz, an infallible instrument of evaluation, standard setter, learners' goal, societal criterion of employment and a necessary evil. Their eminent position in social milieu, key role in educational set up, impact on teaching learning process and omnibus use in selection, teaching learning process for selection and certification of achievement have made examinations a prestigious institution. Their role at different times in different situations can be appreciated if we trace the origin and history in terms of their use.

Perhaps the first evidence of oral examinations is found in the old testament of the pronunciation test the Gileadites gave to their enemies, the Ephraimites, who had escaped to cross the Jorden. If the word "Shibboleth" was pronounced as "Sibboleth" by some one he was identified as Ephraimite and slewn at the passage of Jorden. Socrates used oral quizzing by putting searching questions upto the middle of 19th century as standard oral examinations were used in American schools. Written tests are comparatively of more recent origin but even they date back to 2200 B.C., when Chinese are believed to have had a national system of examinations to select their public servants. First educational tests were like our performance tests when primitive tribes tasted their young men for their endurance, bravery, hunting skills etc. Educational use of written tests was perhaps for the first time used by the University of Cambridge, England in 1702.

One of the earliest records of educational testing in America dates back to the written examination in Boston in the year 1845. Prior to that oral examinations prevailed. During the 19th century three major developments were; popularity of written examination over oral testing; refinement of evaluation devices to ensure more objectivity in measurement and that of comparing performances of bigger groups of students; a step towards development of norms.

Developments during 20th century can be briefly summed up as under:

- Assessment of persons on the basis of written ability,
- Survival skills as basis of testing physical development,
- Written word in preference to oral word for objective measurement,
- Comparative performances for developing group norms,
- Cognizance of tangible and intangible instructional objectives,
- Refinement of tools and techniques of testing,
- Use of statistical methods in educational measurement,

Two major trends observable are broadening of the concept of measurement and making measurement more scientific.

1.2 Development in Pre-independence India

Major recommendations made by various committees, commissions and national policies are given below:

(a) *Wood's Dispatch (1854)*: Institution of entrance examination as a first public examination.

(b) *Resolution of 1913:* Combination of external and internal assessment.

(c) *Hertog's Committee (1920)*: To reduce incidence of failure.

(d) *University Education Commission (1948)*: Appointing full fledged board of examiners and allocation of one third marks for class work.

(e) *Secondary Education Commission Report (1952)*: Introduction of internal assessment data in the certificate and use of symbolic grading.

(f) *Dr. Bloom's Visit (1957)*: Development of 10 years phased programme of examination reform.

(g) *Ministry of Education (1961)*: Establishment of National Council of Educational Research and Training and State Evaluation Units.

(h) *N.C.E.R.T. (1964)*: Rajasthan Board of Secondary Education launches examination reform project in collaboration with N.C.E.R.T.

(i) *Indian Education Commission (1966)*: Recommended comprehensive evaluation of students by using various tools and techniques in internal assessment.

(j) *National Policy on Education (1968)*: Emphasised improvement in quality of measuring instruments and using evaluation to improve students' achievement.

(k) *V.K.R.V. Rao Committee (1974)*: Multiple paper setting and separate indication of internal assessment and public examination performance in the certificate.

(l) *N.C.E.R.T. Curriculum Frame Work for Ten Year School (1975):* Evaluation as a feed back service and strengthening internal assessment programme for ultimate abolishing of external examinations.

(m) *Plus-two Approach Paper, N.C.E.R.T. (1976):* Unit-wise flexible system of 2 to 6 semesters with 7 point grading leading to cumulative credit.

(n) *National Policy on Education (1986):* Integrating evaluation with teaching through continuous, comprehensive assessment in schools.

(o) *Programme of Action (1992):* Ensure valid and reliable measure of students' performance, use of grades in place of marks and setting up of National Evaluation

Organisation to organize nation wide tests for comparability of performance across the states.

(p) *National Curriculum Framework (2000):* School based evaluation to be continuous, comprehensive covering both scholastic and co-scholastic aspects, use of formative evaluation in the form of criterion-referenced testing, diagnostic testing, mastery testing etc. at elementary stage.

(q) *N.C.E.R.T. Curriculum Framework (2005):* Focus on question setting rather than paper setting; elimination of the terms pass/fail by permitting repeated retakes, establishment of school based continuous and comprehensive assessment and keeping internal assessment honest. Purpose of giving selected references of recommendations made during pre-independence and post independence is to take cognizance of the emerging trends in the field of examination reform and make out a case for increasing concern for the school based assessment system and de-emphasising public examinations, making it more transparent, flexible and learner friendly. However, examination reform will attain very little unless it is accompanied by improvement of teacher training to improve quality of teachers. Nevertheless, to hasten reform within Indian education it is the pivotal position of examination reform that can be used to improve the existing conditions. Thus system of examination needs re-examination to make it more trust worthy, humanistic and teacher based.

1.3 Making School Based Assessment more Valid?

One significant reflection emerged out of the various views and recommendations is to de-emphasise the external examinations and replace it with schools based assessment to ensure more validity of learners' assessment. Following reasons support this contention which strengthens the case of school based assessment:

(a) ***The teacher who teaches, alone knows well.***

(i) What part of syllabus or a unit of teaching has been taught well or has not been taught well? (Knowledge of *content validity*)

(ii) What for that content i.e. unit of teaching, was taught or what was the intended learning competencies which he expected the students to develop as a result of teaching? (care of *construct validity*)

(iii) How best the teaching learning experiences were provided or teaching learning competencies adopted to develop those intended learning competencies? (Cognizance of *curricular validity*)

(iv) How best he has taught the content to achieve the intended assessment objectives or how best the students have learnt i.e. they have developed the intended competencies as revealed in evaluation? (Understanding of *empirical validity*)

(v) How best the evidence gathered through evaluation was used by the teacher for further improvement of instructional effectiveness and for improvement of students' achievement? (Reflection of *predictive validity*)

Answer to all these questions (i) to (v) can be traced back to the basic teaching model of Glasser applicable to school based teaching and testing shown below diagrammatically.

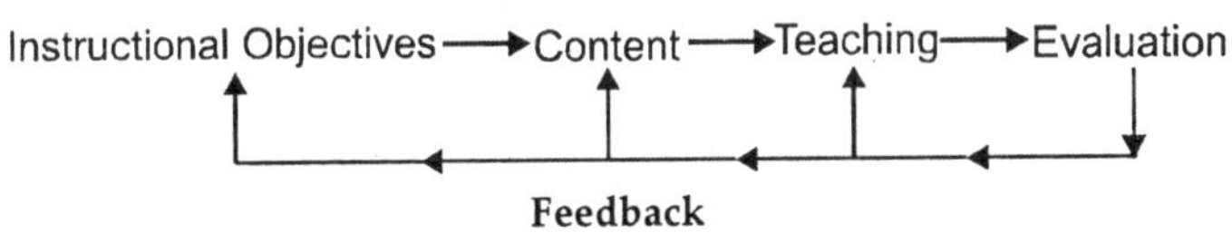

Each of the five questions (i to v) relates to one of the aspects of this model that takes care of different types of validities.

(b) ***It is again the class teacher who alone knows well.***

(i) What is the academic, social and economic background of students?

(ii) What are their limitations and strengths in terms of learning?

(iii) How best to involve students in learning and teaching?

(iv) How best to encourage them in self, peer and class assessment?

(v) How best to use assessment for improvement of pupils' achievement?

(c) *It is again the teacher who knows well.*

(i) How best he can ensure parent's cooperation in improving their wards for developing more interest in learning?

(ii) How best he can develop community support for providing better resources of teaching and learning?

(iii) How best he can utilise learning environments of the school for improving students' learning and his own instruction?

(iv) How best he can make assessment of students' learner friendly to develop positive self-concept among his students?

(d) *It is again the teacher who alone is the best judge to decide.*

(i) What assessment objectives related to a particular unit of teaching are relevant for a particular class?

(ii) When and what co-scholastic aspects can better be assessed during and after school hours and with whose collaboration?

(iii) When and how students can be actively made to participate in their own self-assessment and their peer's assessment?

(iv) How best to integrate evaluation with teaching for continuous assessment and use it for improving their achievement?

If we agree to the above mentioned assertions about teachers' capabilities and develop faith; of course, after proper training and retraining from time to time; we are sure that there would not be any major problem to make internal assessment (S.B.A.) a viable alternative to external examinations which really are necessary evil because of any other credible alternative to these examinations.

1.4 Understanding Role of Assessment Objectives

(a) *Nature, Scope and Derivation of Instructional Objectives*

It hardly needs any mention that all practioners of school-based assessment are supposed to be well versed in the instructional objectives of the subject they teach. However, for reinforcing the basic ideas concerning the role of assessment objectives it seems appropriate to highlight the major concepts, understanding of which help them to make teaching and testing objective based. An objective represents the end point of teaching and testing objective based. An *objective* represents the end point of learning and therefore:

(i) It is a product of learning, *not* a process of learning.

(ii) It is a learning outcome, *not* a learning experience.

(iii) It is an intended outcome of learning, *not* the content of learning. Scope of an objective varies from the most general to the most specific e.g. To develop wholesome personality; to develop pupils' scholastic aspects; to develop observational skills; to develop the ability of adding two digit numbers correctly etc. Thus objectives indicate the intended learning outcomes at different levels.

Objectives can be derived empirically using job analysis technique by identifying significant behaviours or through *critical incidence technique* by noting significant or critical behaviours that enable the learner to do his task well. The other most commonly used technique is the views of curriculum experts. Three sources in this context are learners, society and the discipline concerned. Thus (a) learners' needs and abilities (b) societal demands and pressure (c) requirements of the discipline concerned are the basis for deriving objectives.

(b) *Formulation and Specification of Objectives*

Objectives can be formulated at national, state, stage, subject, unit and at lesson levels. As practicing teacher in the school he is mainly concerned with the formulation of objectives at the subject, unit and lesson level. Objectives can be classified into three main categories in cognitive domain, affective domain and psychomotor domain. In case of written examinations it is the cognitive domain objectives, which are of concern to the practioners. There are a number of taxonomies of educational objectives but the most popular one is the one developed in India by the N.C.E.R.T. after a lot of experimentation in the field. This reflects three objectives in hierarchical order of "Knowledge, Understanding and Application objectives. These objectives are arranged in order of cumulative hierarchy. This means that the lower most objective is *knowledge* which becomes a part of *understanding objective* which in turn becomes a part of *application objective* which is the most complex in the hierarchy. Not going into the details of classification of objectives described in various taxonomies of objectives under cognitive, affective and psychomotor domains let us try to clarify the concept of cumulative hierarchy with respect to the three objectives mentioned above. Suppose Knowledge objective is used to test X, Understanding objective tests Y and Application objective tests Z then it can be expressed as under:

- Knowledge objective can be represented as X
- Understanding objective is represented as X + Y
- Application objective is represented as X + Y + Z

This means that

- when knowledge is tested we test only knowledge objective i.e. only X
- When understanding is tested we test knowledge objective also i.e. both X and Y because knowledge is included in understanding.
- When application is tested we test knowledge as well understanding objectives also since both are included

in the application i.e. X+Y are pre-requisites to Z. Thus we can put it in another way also that X knowledge is = X while understanding is = X + something and Application is X + Y + something.

Thus we can tests students at three levels through written tests depending upon the content elements selected and the purpose of testing. Of course certain content elements like 'term' are usually tested at knowledge level; some at knowledge and understanding levels and still others at all the three levels e.g.; concept of ' osmosis can be tested at three levels. Weightage to these three objectives can be given depending upon the nature and scope of content of testing and instructional objectives being tested.

1.5 Specification of Learning Objectives

Since instructional objectives are Intended Learning Outcomes (ILOs) each objective has to be defined or specified in terms of intended competencies we expect the students to develop as a result of instruction or self-learning. For example in case of *knowledge objective*, the intended competencies or I.L.Os expected are: students' ability to recall, recognize identify, reproduce ......(content elements, concepts, principles etc.).

In case of *Understanding objectives*, intended competencies to be developed (I.L.Os) are students' ability to:

- translate, illustrate, relate, compare, classify, interpret etc.

In case of *Application objective* the intended competencies (I.L.Os) expected to be developed are the ability to:

- analysis, hypothesise, suggest procedures, draw conclusions, predict, evaluate etc.

Purpose of this specification is that while planning his unit plan or a lesson plan the teacher should be able to make list of I.L.Os i.e. the competencies under each assessment objective, he expects the students to develop as a result of his teaching that particular unit. Different units have different scope of developing various competencies.

Intended learning outcomes for each unit or even each lesson can be stated in terms of pupils' behaviours i.e. intended competencies as exemplified below:

At the end of this unit students will be able to:

(a) *Recall*—chemical properties of oxygen gas.
(b) *Translate*—the given population data in the form of a graph.
(c) *Illustrate*—diagrammatically the working of a water pump.
(d) *Compare*—chemical properties of oxygen with that of hydrogen.
(e) *Interpret*—the given graph showing the population for last 20 years.
(f) *Analyse*—the various factors that contribute to growing terrorism.
(g) *Predict*—the likely impact of growing environment pollution on man?

Like-wise other I.L.Os can also be stated depending upon the content elements in a unit. It is the italicised word in each case that reflects I.L.O. or the competency expected to be developed and later on tested to know whether it has developed or not. Thus teaching for developing the intended competencies and then testing for those very competencies to know whether developed or not; is the basic purpose of our assessment objectives. Thus focus of our emphasis is on *competency based* teaching and *competency based testing*.

To Sum up

We have made a peep into the historical developments in the field of testing and examination and their role in the teaching learning process. Developments in pre-independence and post-independence India in the field of examination reform have reflected a number of changing emphases. One significant trend is towards de-emphasising the external examinations and giving more importance to institution based assessment. More emphasis is being given to improve measurement value of examinations by improving quality of tools and techniques of evaluation; using evaluation for improving students' achievement; assessment of total development of the learners flexibility in taking examination and making it learner friendly. And one of the best ways to make it work is to integrate evaluation with teaching and learning which can be possible only through school based assessment system. To undertake this task successfully the practicing teachers must be thoroughly acquainted with the basic concepts, process characteristics and technique of evaluation, discussion of which is taken in the next chapter.

2

Contemporary Concepts in Educational Evaluation

Historical retrospect of examinations in pre-independence and post-independence reveals that unless our examinations provide written record of comprehensive and reliable evidences about learners' total development through association of class teachers by improving the school based assessment system, quality of external examinations can not be improved to the desired extent. Role of examination is not only to measure students' learning but is extended to the improvement of their achievements. New emerging demands on todays' evaluators of more comprehensive evaluation of students and needed expertise for effective evaluation requiring variety of tools and techniques demands that the practicing classroom teachers get acquainted with the new concepts and web of terminology in the field of evaluation. Once the key concepts reflected in the new terminology are understood it would facilitate to use these terms while explaining role of evaluation as an instructional device being an integral part of teaching learning process for better understanding of process characteristics of evaluation and the steps involved in the evaluate process. Since many a terms are interchangeably used by teachers it is desirable that before taking up basic principles of evaluation, nature, scope and purpose of these terms be explained and categorized to reflect inter-relationship. For convenience three-way system of classification is adopted. For want of space details are not given.

2.1 Tripartite Classification of Terms

(a) *Examination, Measurement and Evaluation*

- *Examination*: It is a process of gathering evidences about pupils' learning through data collection using different tools and techniques. It is a process of collecting information, not a tool of testing.
- *Measurement*: According to Lindquist measurement is an act of assigning numerals to an object or an attribute according to certain rules. The attribute may be achievement, intelligence, aptitude, personal or social quality. It deals with how much of a thing. It may be qualitative or quantitative for which some tools are used for measurement e.g. a test, observation schedule etc.
- *Evaluation*: According to Ten Brink evaluation is a process of collecting information and using it to form judgments, which in turn are used for making decisions. Measurement is pre-requisite for evaluation. Measurement is limited to 'how much of a thing' whereas evaluation goes a step further to tell us of what value is that measurement.
  Evaluation = Measurement + Value judgment. (Gronlund)

(b) *Cognitive, Affective and Psychomotor Evaluation:*

- *Cognitive Evaluation*: It relates to testing of intellectual development or cognitive learning outcomes like knowledge, understanding, application etc., which are the usual assessment objectives in our written examinations.
- *Affective Evaluation*: It includes testing of those objectives, which are concerned, with personal and social development of learners like assessment of interests, attitudes, aptitudes, values etc.
- *Psychomotor Evaluation*: It covers the assessment of students on practical work involving experimental

skills like fitting up of an experiment, handling of apparatus etc. that demands assessment of both process and product of performance.

(c) ***Written, Oral and Practical Examinations***

- *Written Examinations*: These are paper pencil examinations and written word is the medium of testing in the form of one or more questions as unit test, term test or annual test. All public examinations are written examinations.
- *Oral Examinations*: Here oral word or viva voce are the medium of response. It may be conducted in the form of oral questions, dialogue, speaking, reading, oral questioning in class, conversation etc.
- *Practical Examinations*: Actual performance is the basis of testing practical, observational, experimental, manipulative, diagrammatic skills, painting, socially useful productive work etc. which form the basis of examination.

(d) ***Internal, External and Exo-internal Evaluation***

- *Internal Evaluation*: All assessment of students undertaken by teachers of an institution who teach those students are internal assessments whether carried out in the school or outside the school. Even when assessment made by a teacher who does not teach those students cannot be termed as internal assessment although it is a school based assessment.
- *External Evaluation:* When students are tested by any examination agency like the boards, directorates of education or any other person who is not connected with instruction of a students and marking is also undertaken under the agencies of examination agency, it is external evaluation.
- *Exo-internal Evaluation:* It envisages combination of both external and internal assessment. For example papers are set externally but scripts are evaluated

internally by the school or papers are set internally by school teachers, not teaching that class but scripts are evaluated by the class teacher or papers are set internally by the class teacher but evaluation is done by teachers not teaching that class or a team of class teachers set and evaluate the scripts.

(e) ***Rational, Formative and Summative***

- *Rational Evaluation:* Its attributes are logic, experience, reasoning and enlightened opinion of evaluators. Initially relevance of objectives, content, instructional strategy and mode of evaluation are mostly judged rationally through consensus of more than one evaluator, experts or subject experts familiar with the task. It is subjective in nature without any empirical basis.
- *Formative Evaluation*: It is an integral part of teaching learning process, usually limited to cognitive learning outcomes. Its focus is on improvement of learning, instruction, development, but not judgmental in nature. Classroom questioning, assignments, teachers' observations and diagnosing pupils' inadequacies in learning are examples of formative evaluation which provides feed back on students' learning and instructional impact involving self-referenced and norm-referenced judgments.
- *Summative Evaluation*: Its purpose is on appraising the end product of instructional efforts and is judgmental in nature; concerned with assessment of I.L.Os of instruction at the end of a semester, session or a course. It refers to worth whileness of an instructional programme and judges its merit to retain or adapt it e.g. annual test, semester-wise testing and public examinations. Its purpose is grading, promotion and certification of achievement. Measurement of achievement, not improvement of achievement is the focus of summative evaluation.

(f) *Self-referenced, Norm-referenced and Criterion-referenced Judgments:*

- *Self-referenced Judgments*: When an individual's performance is compared with his own progress at two different times (now and then) in terms of instructional outcomes or even in terms of ranking in group or class performance and not in terms of criteria but pupil himself to know his progress or retardation. e.g. Arshiya got first position now (3rd last time)
- *Norm referenced Judgments*: These are made in terms of norm group like class, district, state or national level performance, Purpose is to find the extent to which one's performance differs from the norm group he belongs to, as in public examination where judgments are made with reference to the norm group; or class; who got 3rd position? Arshiya's marks are more than 90 per cent of students in her class. These are norm-referenced judgments.
- *Criterion referenced Judgments:* Here judgments are made in terms of specified, acceptable intended level of proficiency stated in terms of well defined criterian behaviours which form the basis of interpreting the results and serves as referents or criteria. At elementary stage where learning of fundamental skills and concepts, is necessary, criterion referenced measurement is relevant. Success of criterion-referenced judgment depends on how well the intended performance criteria are defined.

(g) *Assessment, Appraisal and Testing*

- *Assessment*: It is an approximation of teachers' estimate of value against a certain standard. It is an estimate made about an attribute or aspect of development e.g. assessment of attitudes as against score on an objective test.
- *Appraisal*: Though used interchangeably with assessment and evaluation by teachers but it is

generally defined as an accurate and formal valuation of characteristics against some defined or stipulated criteria against which the worth of an attribute is to be measured e.g. appraisal of a textbook from national integration point of view, criteria for which is worked out by curriculum experts.

- *Testing*: It is one of the most significant and usable techniques of examination or evaluation used to collect information or evidence needed for assessment or appraisal. Testing involves use of tools for collecting information. Question paper is one of the most potent tools used in case of written examination to get information about pupils' achievement.

(h) ***Formal Non-Formal and Informal Evaluation***

- *Formal Evaluation*: It is planned and highly structured process of evaluation representing official mode. All steps are well defined and conventionalized. Evaluation tools are set in advance and judgments are made in terms of established norms, focus being on grading, classification and certification of pupils e.g. public examinations, selection tests, standardized tests etc.
- *Non-Formal Evaluation:* It is neither well structured nor institutionalized and used in non-formal education. Non-formal tests are need based and adjustable in terms of need and progress of individuals or subgroups usually educated through methods other than formal schooling e.g. adult education classes and corresponding courses.
- *Informal Evaluation*: It is unintended, unstructured, unplanned and untimed free from fobia of formal examinations. It goes on during classroom teaching like questioning, assignments, observers' reflective judgments, unannounced testing etc. It is indeed a part of classroom teaching and its scope and frequency is not determinable.

(i) *Product Process and Product-cum-Process Evaluation*

- *Product Evaluation*: It is concerned with appraisal of intended outcomes, yield, outputs, an end product or results. Though product and process both are considered for evaluation, here we limit to appraisal of only product of performance as in the case of science practicals, wood work, typing and performing arts etc. Quality and speed are basic criteria of assessment.
- *Process Evaluation*: It involves various steps or inquiry processes to develop the intended product or output. Operational steps like measuring, classifying, inferring, predicting etc. which are also called process objectives, are tested in process evaluation. Such processes vary from simple observing to relevant tools or apparatus to the most complex experimental set up or developing a model plan.
- *Product-cum-Process Evaluation*: Both process and product complement each other and both are equally important. In certain cases process is more important as in case of identifying a salt in chemistry where a number of steps are involved. In other cases product is more important as in a finished product like a model or a painting. Process evaluation is formative while product evaluation is summative in nature.

(j) *Objective Based, Goal free and Pay off Evaluation*

- *Objectives Based Evaluation*: It envisages formulation and specification of instructional objectives. Its fócus is on determination of the degree to which intended objectives are achieved and reflects the adequacies and inadequacies of instructional programmes. Evidences are collected in terms of stated objectives and judgments are also made in terms of goals or specified objectives.
- *Goal free Evaluation*: Most of the class room evaluations are goal free and are concerned more with instructional effects than formal instructional objectives i.e. decisions

taken relate more to the observed objectives than formal stated objectives. Thus evaluator is encouraged to take care of wider range of outcomes of a programme.

- *Pay off Evaluation*: This term used by Scriven, is the outcome of the judgmental model involving intrinsic (process) or extrinsic (product) criteria. It relates to programme effects in contrast to intrinsic criteria that concern internal characteristics of an instructional programme. Most of the empirical investigations use extrinsic criteria for judgementing and therefore, are pay off evaluation. It may or may not be goal oriented but leans on assessment of dividends.

(k) *Quantitative, Qualitative and Responsive Evaluation*

- *Quantitative Evaluation*: It refers to the assignment of numerals to any attribute of personality of the individual whose achievement is recorded in the form of scores represented by some kind of numbers i.e. assignment of numerals to an object of measurement. Testing is the main source of data for quantitative evaluation. Written examinations and other forms of testing yield scores called raw scores amenable to manipulation into various forms. Judgments are mostly norm-referenced.
- *Qualitative Evaluation*: Here mode of appraisal is qualitative, sometimes called non-measurement of the attributes of measurement, which are difficult to measure quantitatively e.g. personal social qualities like civic sense, patriotism, intellectual honesty etc. Here underlying principle is that attribute can only be assessed in terms of degree or extent of its growth or achievement on a continuum e.g. letter grading, ranking, verbal description etc. Tools and techniques usable are observation, rating scale, check list, etc. which do not yield scores. In contrast to quantitative evaluation it yields subjective data due to lack of well developed criterion behaviours and, therefore, most

appropriate judgments are self-referenced, not norm-referenced.

- *Responsive Evaluation*: According to Robert Stake it is oriented more to the programme activity than programme intents and responds to requirements of the audience for information, by engaging different observers to observe and negotiate the programme and prepare the narratives, graphs etc. Accuracy of portrayals and reactions with audience members is checked and recorded. Rather than the objectives, he prefers to identify issues which reflect better the complexity, immediacy and valuing of the programme. It is these issues, which are basic for information gathering, making observations, conduct interviews and tests. Evaluator consults teachers, students, parents and other programme staff to identify issues or potential problems. Its limitation is uncertainly and ambiguity of reports. Responsive evaluation is a new approach of cooperative enterprises in evaluating a programme.

(l) ***Rational, Experimental and Illuminative Evaluation***

- *Rational Evaluation*: It is also called logical evaluation since the evaluator forms his judgment on some logic he uses as the basis. Reasoning, logic, experience and personal experience and values preferred are the main attributes of rational evaluation. It is purely subjective without any empirical basis. As criteria adopted may not be agreeable more than one evaluators are involved who are conversant with the task to be evaluated. Basic tenet underlying this evaluation is finding out the relevance of material on the basis of experienced expertise. Judgments involve reflection on the predetermined nodal points. It is the most popularly acclaimed method of evaluation usable in most of the situations relating to the educational process.
- *Experimental Evaluation*: Based on classical paradigm derived from experimental and mental testing

traditions in psychology it utilizes hypothetical deductive methodology. This approach yields objective numerical data, which permits statistical analysis. It involves control of variables in the pre-experiment. Achievement testing, intelligence testing, development of attitude scales, interest inventories and personality inventories are examples of experimental evaluation. Main limitation is controlling of variables and tends to be more centralized and bureaucratic 'in decision making process'.

- *Illuminative Evaluation*: In contrast to classical paradigm it is based on social anthropological participant observation research. Trow (1970) used this term to take care of wider context in which a programme functions. Focus is on description and interpretation rather than on measurement and evaluation. It aims at studying how a programme operates and is influenced by different school situations and documents like a participant in the scheme. It illuminates a variety of questions having bearing on process of education. Two main concepts central to understand the illuminative evaluation are the 'instructional system' and the 'learning milieu', emphasis being more on 'process' of learning rather than on 'outcomes' of learning Observation, opinion, discussion and interview schedule are main tools. Appraisal of complex interaction of various parameters that impact pupils' learning and forming judgments' on the basis of consensus of all those who are participants in teaching learning process reflect illuminative evaluation.

In short description of web of evaluation related terminology used was followed by its classification into different categories made on the basis or the criterion used. For example we can have; objective, subjective and participatory, rational, empirical and consensus; self, teacher and institutional evaluation; autocratic, bureaucratic and democratic etc. Purpose was to enable the teachers with different data collecting devices, mode of judgementing and decision focus. Three major attributes of evaluation emphasised are; 'intended learning outcomes, outputs and impact', relevance, reliability and usability of evidences, value judgment, decision focus and accountability.

2.2 Basic Principles of Educational Evaluation

We have already discussed in the last chapter that evaluation is an integral part of school curriculum which reflects the totality of learning experiences for which a school undertakes the responsibility to achieve the pre-determined goals through continuous appraisal of both process of learning and product of learning. It was in this context that basic teaching model of Glasser was described showing the interrelationship of objectives, content, method or teaching learning strategies and evaluation with feedback on all components. For adapting and improving intended objectives, content selected, instructional strategies and even evaluation process.

(a) *Fundamental Bases of the Concept*

This simple model reflects the five fundamental bases of the concept of evaluation.

- (i) Evaluation is objective focused with purpose being the improvement of students' achievement and teaching learning process (Philosophical basis).
- (ii) Emphasis on equality of performance standard, using minimum bands of classification and focus on 80 per cent students to attain standard which now 25 per cent attain (social basis).
- (iii) Using examination or tests for diagnosing weaknesses and remediation, provide sense of success and rewarding experiences to develop positive self-concept among students to improve their achievement (Psychological basis).
- (iv) For collecting dependable evidences measuring tools and techniques must ensure validity and reliability of

scores by making measurement relevant to instructional objectives, yield dependable scores and use of competency based criterion referenced judgments (Scientific basis).

(v) Making evaluation integral part of teaching and learning; pupil, curriculum and programme evaluation as inter related processes and using evaluation as feed back device for quality control of curriculum instruction and students' learning i.e. growth oriented (Ecological basis).

(b) *Three Basic Principles*

These principles can be identified on the basis of certain assumptions about the learners and the information gathering process as given below:

(i) *Learners have measurable ability:* Intelligence and ability to apply in an individual can be estimated through observation or in terms of true scores as per measurement theory.

(ii) *Observation contains error*: Observation does not yield true score. Error is more in psychological measurement than in physical measurement.

(iii) *Observed score minus error score is true score*: We can write this assumption as $X = t \pm e$ It means:
Observed score = True score ± Error score.

(c) ***Principles about error***

(i) Errors can be identified.
(ii) Errors can be minimized.
(iii) Errors can be estimated.
(iv) Errors can be lived with.

2.3 Basic Characteristics of Evaluation

(a) *It is objective based:* In every subject instructional objectives are started in the curriculum to indicate the intended learning outcomes at different stages in terms of cognitive, affective and psychomotor outcomes of learning. These objectives are usually specified in terms of pupils' behaviour or competencies to be developed as a result of teaching and learning. Therefore, purpose, objective, value, criterion or success indicator; etc are basic to make evaluation objective centred. However, now different models like 'goal free; "issue based, "pay off," illuminative, etc. described earlier are also available.

(b) *It is a continuous process*: During teaching learning process when different competencies are being developed it is necessary to judge side by side the adequacies and inadequacies in their learning to adapt instructional strategies and provide feedback to students. Thus assessment of performance becomes integrated with instruction. For that evaluation questions are used at pre-instructional stage to find readiness of students for placement; using questions as teaching device during instructional phase by questioning in class to get feedback about students' learning and instructional impact; and using assignments and unit testing at post instructional phase for judging how far intended objectives of the unit of teaching are achieved.

(c) *It is a comprehensive process:* Assessment of both scholastic and co-scholastic aspects is necessary for judging total development of learners for which different tools and techniques of evaluation are used. Comprehensiveness in terms of intended objectives, coverage of syllabus and content elements to get evidence on all aspects of pupils' development is essential using all possible sources of proper judgmenting about pupils' achievement.

(d) *It is a cooperative process*: In order to collect evidences about various scholastic and co-scholastic aspects of pupils' development teachers have to use various types of tools and techniques like tests, attitude scales, interest and personality inventories etc. For that peers, parents and other teachers, counsellors and others, who have seen the learner, grow are to be consulted for making good judgments about the learners. Thus evaluation is a cooperative process.

(e) *It is an integral part of teaching*: In a way evaluation is a service component of the teaching learning process and not an end-of-the—course activity as reflected in the teaching model discussed earlier. Its focus is on diagnosis and feed back i.e. formative in nature.

(f) *It is a dynamic process*: Evaluation provides evidences about the attainability of intended or stated objectives, suitability of the content selected or concepts included in a unit or in a syllabus; on the instructional impact or instructional strategies and even about the quality of evaluation instrument (test/question paper). Thus it generates dynamic interaction among all the components of teaching learning process and validates them.

It is evident that evaluation is no longer a process of testing but its focus is on improving students' learning, instruction and acting as intelligence service of teaching learning process.

2.4 Steps Involved in Process of Evaluation

Following steps are involved in carrying evaluation successfully:

(a) *Specifying intended learning outcomes*: Foremost decision in a programme of evaluation is the purpose of evaluation which may be selection; placement, diagnosis, certification of achievement etc. Thus first step is to develop the instructional objectives and defining them in terms of intended learning competencies expected to be developed as a result of good teaching and learning. These objectives become the basis for teaching and testing and reference points for validating the evidences collected.

(b) *Assessing pre-requisite learning*: Evaluation being integral part of teaching learning process testing of students' readiness during pre-instructional phase become necessary to know whether they have acquired the knowledge and skills considered necessary as pre-requisite for learning the topic in hand. If adequate, developmental teaching goes on; if inadequate then remedial teaching is undertaken to make them ready for developmental teaching. Thus evaluation is formative.

(c) *Devising relevant situations for testing:* Once I.L.O.'s are specified and students' readiness is ensured next step is to collect evidences for which situations are devised. These may become a particular activity e.g. drawing a diagram; a project, a field trip, library visit, science exhibition, games or sports, quizzes, debates, discussions are the most usable situation of testing. Selection of situation depends on the intended learning outcomes to be tested like intellectual abilities, skills, interests, habits, attitudes, personality trait, social adjustment etc. Testing is the most acceptable situation for assessment of cognitive outcomes to get more valid and reliable evidence and may take the form of oral, written or practical exercises.

(d) *Obtaining the needed evidences*: Next step is to obtain evidences. Following four substages (according to Ten Brink (1975), are as under:

(i) *Find information already available*: This is possible from various sources like record of previous achievements, parents' opinion, cumulative record etc. Relevance of information to purpose and its accuracy is important.

(ii) *How to gather information?*: Depending upon the type of evidence any of the four basic techniques can be used., namely; testing, enquiry, observation and analysis. Different types of tools or instruments of evaluation like a test, observation schedule, questionnaire are there.

(iii) *Construction or selection of instruments:* It is to be ensured that instruments selected or constructed are valid and reliable.

(iv) Administer tools and techniques for gathering evidences: For good administration teachers should be well prepared in terms of time limit, invigilation, relevance of instructions, formatting questions, scoring etc.

(e) *Analysing and recording of data:* Three modes of analysis are:

- *Norm referenced*: Students' achievement is judged with reference to his class, school, a district or state board like C.B.S.E. i.e. against a norm or average performance of the group he belongs to.
- *Criterion-referenced*: Here performances of pupils' is analysed in terms of pre-determined criteria like instructional objectives i.e. intended learning outcomes. Criteria varies with attribute being tested; for example in case of mastery of fundamental concepts or a spelling test it is 80 per cent or more considered desirable, (not 40% or 33%). This type of analysis is done in terms of an individual with reference to stipulated criteria of performance.
- *Self-referenced*: Self-referenced analysis in terms of his own effort or ability or experiential background, not in terms of any norm.

(f) *Forming Judgments and decision taking*: Analysis is followed by interpretation of evidences to form judgments like grading, diagnosing, predicting future success etc. and decision are taken about detentions, remediation, promotions etc, It may be deviation judgments, mastery judgments or predictive judgments. Decision taking is the ultimate aim of evaluation and therefore, judgments need to be verified to avoid wrong decisions, which defeats the very purpose of collecting evidences about pupils' Learning. Therefore, whenever decision is taken about grading, remediation, change in instructional strategy or certification, teachers should clearly specify their objective in terms of expected learning outcomes of these alternatives; visualize likely consequences of each course of action and choose the best alternative and probable outcomes with appropriate weightage.

(g) *Summarising and reporting of data or evidences*: Summarising involve preparation of evaluation reports and communicating them to their users. It helps further decisions by teachers, parents, administrators and other clientele. Mode of summarisation depends on the use to which report is to be put. Reporting should include all minimum essential information for intended users in easy to understand manner. In fact reporting is regarded as a service component of evaluation process on whose basis relation is established between teachers, parents and students, making it participatory evaluation.

2.5 Providing Feedback and Needed Correctives

Feedback mechanism provides loop to each component of the teaching learning process as shown diagrammatically in the Glasser model in figure on page 5. Feedback can be utilised in different ways like the following:

(i) *Judging the efficacy of the instructional objectives:* When the results are analysed in terms of instructional objectives and in terms of specific learning outcomes i.e. competencies, it is possible to form the basis for addition, deletion or modification of certain outcomes depending upon students' performance in a given subject for a class.

(ii) *Improving the prescribed syllabus:* Analysis of evidences would reveal inadequacies in terms of difficulty level of certain topics, under-emphasis of certain areas or misplacement of concepts requiring further investigation regarding review of existing syllabus.

(iii) *Promoting student's learning*: Analysis of performance on various concepts reflect direction for further improvement in view of existing level of students' performance and that helps to motivate for further learning and development of positive self-concept.

(iv) *For improving instruction*: Students' performance on tests indicates instructional impact on students' performance and that helps to motivate further learning strategies in respect of unit of learning and form the basis for improving instruction.

(v) *For providing guidance*: Results indicate success or failure on the basis of which future performance of students can be predicated. On the basis of poor performance and identification of weaknesses in various areas and subjects guidance can be provided for selecting right courses, besides providing individualised instruction and enrich programmes.

(vi) *For promoting research*: Problems like choice of questions, use of different forms of questions and allotment of marks can be solved through undertaking action (class room) research and using the data for improving instruction and students' learning; This feedback is the last step.

To Conclude

Use of terminology web and its tripartite classification given is useful for understanding the nature, purpose and scope of major concepts related to evaluation. Nature and focus of evaluation is determined by reflecting its philosophical, social, psychological, scientific and ecological bases. Basic principles of measurements highlight the errors in measurement. Process characteristics indicate that evaluation is a continuous, comprehensive, cooperative, integrative and objective based process that engenders dynamic interaction among the various components of instructional system. Steps involved in evaluation process include specification of intended learning outcomes, testing for readiness, devising relevant situations collecting data or evidences, analysing and recording evidences, interpreting, forming judgments, summarizing, reporting of evidences and providing feedback to review, improve and validate the different components of teaching learning process. In view of nature, purpose and scope evaluation can be considered as a total school concept. To what extent and in what way evaluation process can best be used in school based assessment, can be understood better when we are clear about the philosophy and objectives of the school based assessment, taken up in the next chapter.

3

Philosophy Underlying School Based Assessment

Before taking up the philosophy let me once again clarify that use of Word 'Internal assessment' cannot be used as synonymous with School Based Assessment (S.B.A.). Every internal assessment is nitched in the S.B.A. system since it is undertaken by the teacher who teaches his class, not even by an other school teacher who does not teach that particular class because he alone knows well what has been taught and how well has been taught or learnt by his pupils. On the other hand what has been taught, who has taught, and for what purpose the lesson was taught is immaterial for school based assessment system because during the whole year various types of assessments are made at different times by different teachers and even together by more than one teacher. For example we undertake readiness tests for placement; unit tests for formative purpose to get feedback about instructional impact; diagnostic tests to identify pupils' weaknesses or hard spots of learning; criterion—referenced tests for mastery testing; summative tests for classification, judgementing, promotion, certification etc. It is in this context that I prefer to use the terminology of S.B.A., which is more comprehensive and includes internal assessment. Scope of S.B.A. may be restricted to testing of even a single concept like 'Osmosis' in biology course can be tested at various levels varying from simple recall to different competencies under various instructional objectives. Scope may extend to a module, a unit of learning, a section or area of study like Physiology (in a term test) or even the whole syllabus through summative annual examination. Keeping in view this concept, purpose and scope of S.B.A. following is the philosophy of S.B.A. visualized:

3.1 Faith and Conviction in Teachers' Competence

It is indeed unfortunate that we recruit qualified teachers as per requirement of the discipline concerned with a view that they are potentially capable to teach a particular subject to a particular class but once they are in job we trust them for good teaching but not for assessment. We blame them for subjective assessment, which indeed is their right. Unless we cultivate faith in their competence as well as their right to assess their wards we cannot make S.B.A. a reality. If we feel they are more subjective than desired then we can devise ways and means to make their assessment more dependable. Therefore, the foremost viewpoint that contributes to the philosophy of S.B.A. is developing full faith in teachers' competence to assess their wards and their right to form judgment about them.

3.2 Concern for Holistic Assessment and Formative Evaluation

It is only through S.B.A. that we get regular feed back during instruction using various modes like questioning in class at various phases of instruction. This feedback provides evidences about pupils' learning as also instructional effectiveness, thereby, ensuring better learning and instructional impact. This concern for regular improvement of pupils' learning and adapting instructional strategies is possible only through teacher based assessments in the school.

Since focus of good teaching and learning is on total development of the learner it is necessary that there should be holistic assessment of the learners' development; Good affective outcomes improve cognitive learning and holistic assessment provides good clues for improved learning. Limiting assessment to cognitive outcomes provides partial evidences about learners' development and that creates gap between the intended and the observed learning outcomes. This may lead to wrong decisions based on incomplete evidences. Focus of assessment in S.B.A. is on assessment of learners' total development.

3.3 Concern for Competency Based Criterion-Referenced Testing

Concern for mastery learning especially in case of basic concepts and skills at elementary stage is essential to develop intended learning competencies. In contrast to norm-referenced testing where learners' performance is compared with the group he belongs to, focus of S.B.A. is on the intended learning outcomes of the unit of learning. In other words focus remains on assessment of learners' achievement in terms of intended competencies developed during teaching and learning. Based on the evidences collected reporting can be done in terms of observed competencies that forms the basis for further improvement of learners' equality of learning by laying down the levels of learning in terms of achievement targets in the form of acceptable performance indicators.

3.4 Concern for Diagnostic Testing and Remedial Instruction

Since formative evaluation is an integral part of instruction teachers get feed back about inadequacies in pupils' learning which provides the basis for remedial instruction. This may be individualized or group based remedial teaching. When certain hard spots are identified in a particular area or unit of study and area not being remedied by usual class room remedial instruction then on the basis of such hard spots of learning diagnostic tests are constructed in that area and pupils' performance is analysed to determine the causes of weakness followed by relevant remedial measures. Underlying philosophy is to improve pupils' achievement through proper diagnosis that is possible in S.B.A

3.5 School Based Assessment—A Total School Concept

Students' learning or achievement is not only the outcome of the instructional process but is conditioned by various factors that impact learning environments of the school. It may be school setting, in put resources like financial or academic, facility of curriculum transactions, quality of output measures and role of stakeholders of the institution. Therefore, every S.B.A. is school specific and should be interpreted accordingly. Focus is on realization of the need for assessing pupils' achievement and instructional impact in the light of total school environments.

3.6 Conceptualisation of Belief and Practice of S.B.A.

All documents, reports and recommendations of experts' committees from University Education Commission (1948) onward upto the latest N.C.E.R.T. Curriculum Framework (2005) have highlighted the need for more valid teachers' assessments by establishing a sound system of school based assessment. No one can deny that S.B.A. is the only alternative to complement pupils' record of achievement in external examination for making certification more meaningful for admissions, selections and for employment. However, what has been witnessed over the years is the dichotomy in philosophy and practice of S.B.A. (C.C.E.).

(a) Inspite of inbuilt credibility and faith in teachers' assessment in S.B.A. and respecting their integrity and trusting them as real agent of reform, we openly blame them for their subjective judgments. Can we really trust them fully and at the same time blame them for partial and unfair judgments and feel satisfied by allocating 20 per cent, 25 per cent or 30 per cent marks for internal assessment? Is this not a breach of trust?

(b) Compared to external examinations S.B.A. or C.C.E. is considered more valid and reliable measure of pupils' growth yet we prefer to moderate their assessments against external examination assessments which are not always more reliable.

(c) Assessment of total growth of pupils is the sine-qua-non of C.C.E. vis-a-vis S.B.A. No system of S.B.A. can be visualized without assessment of co-scholastic aspects of pupils' development. Inspite of that we find that that co-scholastic aspects are mostly not included, being difficult to assess and seldom considered for certification of pupils.

(d) Internal assessment envisages preference for *descriptive illuminative approach* using teachers' observations, peer evaluation, parents' views and opinion of other participant observers, besides testing. In reality these non-testing techniques are lost sight of in actual practice and application of psychometric methods are considered more appropriate for interpretation and reporting of pupil performance.

(e) Testing for mastery learning through criterion referenced testing is emphasized in C.C.E. to improve performance level of students rather than ranking them by comparison using norm-referenced testing which still prevails with pass at 33, 35, 40 per cent marks as the yard stick.

(f) *Cooperative testing* and evaluation considered necessary for comprehensive assessment of pupils remains in theory as involvement of students, parents and community is rarely practiced. Teacher alone is considered as the sole artibitrator for assessing his pupils.

(g) Letter grades are considered more reliable for labeling students in formative testing because of various measurement errors that creep in quantitative assessment. Inspite of that numerical marks are used mostly as the basis for grading students. Even when letter grades are used it is awarded via the marks.

(h) School based assessment or C.C.E. is school specific because of varying learning environments of each school, which leads to variation in pupils' performance in different institutions. Yet we use various statistical measures to minimize inter-school variance in performance of students.

To Sum up

From the foregoing analysis of what is accepted in theory and what is actually practiced in schools we are in a position to observe stark reality of dichotomous thinking of decision makers who apparently believe in the philosophy of school based assessment but are not prepared to shed off the existing practices which are not compatible with its philosophy. To undertake or put into practice what we believe in theory or philosophy of internal assessment to establish a sound system of internal assessment, the dichotomies now observed between theory and practice are to be conceptualized by the decision makers and practitioners of S.B.A. system.

Once above mentioned dichotomies of theory and practice of S.B.A. are properly conceptualized it is possible to make the intended S.B.A. system a success. As reflected earlier in the description of underlying philosophy, the publically acceptable, professionally credible and administratively feasible S.B.A. will be one in which there is maximum cooperation, participation and integration among the various stakeholders. Therefore, what is needed is how best to ensure maximum involvement to utilize the services of teachers, learners, parents, administrators and community in various decision making processes to make assessment more credible and help pupils to improve their achievement besides enriching school environments to boost teachers' morale and develop faith in their assessment. Once we accept this philosophy of S.B.A. we can delineate the intended objectives of S.B.A.

4

Intended Objectives of School Based Assessment

4.1 Cognizance of Intended Learning Outcomes

It hardly needs any mention that more often than not evaluation is used as an end of the course activity to measure students' achievement in the form of a unit test, term test and annual test. Thus focus of measurement remains on judgementing about pupils' learning and using that for making various decisions. Advantage of school based assessment is that whatever the mode of assessment if they know how well they can make evaluation a teaching learning device. In contrast to external assessment S.B.A. has the advantage of integrating evaluation with teaching learning process and use it as a feed back device to improve instruction and students' learning. To achieve this objective teachers must be well acquainted with the Intended Learning Outcomes (I.L.Os) or success indicators to judge that they have been able to integrate well evaluation with the instructional process. Therefore, to judge this it is expected that teachers would be able to:

(a) use assessment for pre-requisite learning to diagnose inadequacies and undertake remedial teaching if required, for proper placement of students for developmental teaching.

(b) use oral questions during developmental teaching of getting regular feedback about students' learning and adapt teaching for remedial purpose, if required.

(c) use higher order questions during teaching to encourage students to put them also higher order questions, which indirectly indicate that they are understanding the content of teaching related to desired competencies.

(d) construct school and home assignments using higher order questions to get feedback about students' learning vis-à-vis instructional impact.

(e) encourage learners' responses during instruction, which provide needed feedback for further improvement in their learning/achievement.

(f) analyse students' responses during class questioning to identify their weaknesses and provide individual or group based remedial measures.

(g) provide maximum possible opportunity to learners for self-learning and self-assessment to make them active participant learners.

(h) involve students in developing unit-based questions they would like to ask the teachers, about the answer of which they are not sure. Pooling of such questions with proper classification can lead to a non-confidential question pool for later use as source material for testing.

If teachers are able to develop above listed abilities they are doing their best to integrate evaluation with teaching learning process, and are using it to improve instruction and students' learning.

4.2 Ensuring Acceptability of S.B.A. by Stake Holders of Reform

This is perhaps the most significant objective from the point of view of making the scheme a success. Under philosophy of S.B.A. wherein we have accepted internal assessment as a total school concept it is essential that all those like learners, teachers, principals, parents, administers, guidance councellors and community who are concerned with improvement of achievement of students demand improvement in the social learning milieu of the school. Therefore, all the stakeholders first understand fully what S.B.A. system mean and in what way it can prove to be a better system of assessment to cultivate full faith and conviction by all stake holders, measures like the following can be taken:

Monitoring and Evaluation of the Scheme

A high level committee may be established in the directorate of education of each state. This committee may consist of representatives of all stakeholders of reform. The committee may be entrusted with tasks like the following:

(a) Produce written material about the merits of the alternative scheme of S.B.A. (in contrast to external assessment) and circulate for public consumption to get and provide needed feedback.
(b) To collect information about successful implementation of intended projects undertaken by various institutions or other researches, on improving instructional impact and students' learning; for wider dissemination among teachers and other stake holders of reform.
(c) To institute a quarterly journal for diffusion and dissemination of latest resource material on S.B.A. and other research material supporting S.B.A. besides other successful S.B.A. practices leading to improvement of students' performance and instructional practices.
(d) To hold annual intra-state meetings of heads of the institutions to share their experiences problems, experiences and other academic issues for further improvement of their instructional strategies and assessment practices.
(e) To undertake studies and investigations relating to their actual problems of assessment and feed back the results to the monitor and evaluation committee. Besides that, feedback from the stakeholders got through questionnaires and other relevant techniques, about the acceptability of the intended scheme of school based assessment, is useful.

(f) To find ways and means to make the school based assessment system more fair, just and reliable through discussions among teachers, students' reactions, opinion of parents and views of evaluation experts.

(g) To develop and use accountability criteria for teachers using democratic, humanistic and illuminative evaluation approach for providing efficient and fair system of assessing students' achievement. Such criteria may of course be intrinsic (learners' view and reactions) or it may be extrinsic in the form of awards or other incentives or disincentives. Teachers' involvement is necessary in developing such criteria.

4.3 Gathering more Valid and Comprehensive Evidences about Students' Holistic Development

This is the most significant objective of S.B.A. system. No external examination can undertake valid assessment of learners' development of co-scholastic aspects whereas validity of S.B.A. is unquestionable for measurement of co-scholastic aspects. Moreover when holistic development of learners is recommended in educational parlance, holistic assessment also becomes imperative and it is again possible through S.B.A. Teachers who teach and develop those co-scholastic aspects are alone the real masters to assess for development of those very traits. Who else can gather more valid evidences about holistic development of their own students? Besides academic achievement students' study habits, interests in academic activities, positive attitudes towards teachers, other personal and social qualities are equally important as outcomes of learning which play important role in improving cognitive learning outcomes. Focus is therefore, on developing such situations for assessment of total development of students that makes S.B.A. system as valid as possible. To make it a practical reality it is expected that teachers would be able to take the following measures:

(a) Develop in collaboration with evaluation experts a

yearly plan of *Intended Performance Indicators* (I.P.I.) of students' achievement in each subject area covering both cognitive and non-cognitive aspects of development in conformity with prescribed syllabus.

(b) Ensure *construct validity* while assessing the holistic development of students who have undergone relevant learning experiences during the course of studies and reflect assessment of intended competencies.

(c) Develop and use various modes and techniques of assessment relevant to assessment objectives.

(d) Ensure proper coverage of content in terms of elements like concepts, principles, processes and generalizations that form the substantive structure of the subject concerned, essential for *content validity.*

(e) Ensure proper coverage of intended stated assessment objectives, by covering a good sample of learning competencies implied in various objectives, of course assuming that teachers have developed such competencies during teaching process. If this is ensured we are taking care of *curricular validity.*

(f) Analyse the results of students once or twice a year in terms of assessment objectives to know how best our students have done in terms of various stated intended learning outcomes. This provides evidence on the discrepancy or the congruence between the intended and the observed outcomes and that provides this basis for reviewing the intended learning outcomes and/or instructional strategies.

(g) Undertake some studies about their students' performance after the course, when same students appear in other tests like an admission test or selection test like national talent search etc. to judge as to how far their performance in S.B.A. system tallies with their performance in selection test for admission to higher studies or other tests like C.A.T., N.T.S. etc. If it conforms, it reveals good quality testing by teachers in S.B.A. as it reflects *predictive validity* of testing in SBA.

4.4 Making *Assessment* More *Democratic* and Learner Friendly

(a) *Towards Participative and Illuminative Approach*

One of the trends in educational assessment is to make assessment process more democratic. At present even teacher based assessment are usually autocratic in the sense that it is only the teacher's prerogative and right to assess and grade students without involving any other participant observer. To make it democratic we have to make it a cooperative venture by involving all those who are concerned with the achievement of learners and watch them grow through out the year. Since learning takes place not only in the class room but in different situations inside as well as outside the class room and it is not possible for concerned teachers alone to assess learners' performance on all the aspects, especially the co-scholastic aspects unless opinion, observations of learners' themselves, their peers and views of other participant observes are taken. On the basis of inadequate evidence on total development of the learners, validity of teachers' assessment can be questioned. Thus democratic approach not only provides more comprehensive assessment but also gives insight into the various problems and issues relating to students' learning. Considered opinion, views and observations of all participant observers make S.B.A. more valid and reliable on the basis of which better judgments can be formed and right timely decisions taken about students' performance and teaching learning strategies.

Making school based assessment more illuminative reflects social anthropological paradigm and concerned with description and interpretation of evidence rather measurement and prediction. How does a programme work and influenced by varied school situations it attempts to document as a participant in this scheme. School learning milieu and instructional system are two basic concepts underlying illuminative evaluation. Conditions' constraints and those involved in the process are the intended parameters of this evaluation. Subjective estimates, face-to-face discussions, consensus of opinion and descriptive judgment are the characteristics features of illuminative evaluation. It represents social approach based on appraisal of complex interaction of various factors having bearing on pupils' learning. Therefore, if teachers succeed in making S.B.A. *democratic and illuminative* they are able to:

(i) appreciate that school learning milieu and impact of instructional system are basic to S.B.A. reflecting social anthropological paradigm.
(ii) realize that description and interpretation of students' performance is more important than measurement and prediction, and understand how role of participant observers in assessment helps to improve quality of assessment of students.
(iii) incorporate subjective estimates and consensus of participant observers for more realistic and rational judgments about learners' achievement.
(iv) involve all stakeholders of reform for comprehensive assessment of total development of learners.
(v) gather pooled opinion of various observes at different times to diagnose inadequacies in students' learning and take timely action to improve their achievement.
(vi) get regular feedback about students' learning and instructional impact from different participant observers like co-teachers, learners, supervisors, counsellors, parents etc. to self-evaluate and adopt corrective measures for further instructional improvement.

(b) ***Establishing Learner Friendly System***

This objective is well reflected in the new curriculum framework by focus group on examination reform. The idea behind this assertion is that at no stage the pupils should feel discouraged and demotivated that they are under achievers, poor performers, deviants, poor learners or failures. Therefore, neither during instruction nor during assessment of students, whether formative or summative, they are to be dubbed as underachievers or poor performers. What is needed is to find out the causes of their poor performance, be empathetic provide learning resources and additional time for remedial instruction. Instead of pointing out their weakness, their better performance in whatever area or activity has to be appreciated in the class to encourage them for still better performance.

Attempt should be made to encourage their good efforts and ignore reflecting on their poor performance in the class. If teachers are really convinced of learner friendly system of S.B.A. they should be able to take measures like the following:

(i) Not declare students as failures or underachievers but only reflect on the need for working more hard in specified area or topic.

(ii) Not compare performance of poor performers with those of better performers, rather compare with their own previous performance.

(iii) Not insist on a particular date for summative testing like term, or annual test but allow such students to take more time and appear after some days when they feel ready for the examination.

(iv) Use analysis of students' performance in formative testing for remedial teaching and for feedback on instructional impact, rather than grading students for unwarranted comparison.

(v) Encourage self-evaluation by students by providing them unit based exemplar material or even through peer evaluation.

(vi) Organize special session of poor or underachievers to conduct oral testing on pre-announced units of syllabus for on the spot remediation and reinforcement of learning.

(vii) Actively involve students in taking decisions about time frame, mode of assessment and unit of assessment whenever any programme of assessment is undertaken and reporting to be made in terms of intended learning outcomes, not in terms of class performance.

4.5 Improving *Pedagogical Value of Measurement*

(a) *Use Evidence for Improving Teaching Learning Process*

A good system of assessment is concerned with both-improvement of measurement value as well as pedagogical value of measurement. Focus of former is on the improvement of validity and reliability of the measuring instruments or devices to collect relevant and reliable evidences about pupils' learning or achievement. Emphasis of all public examinations and selection tests is on this aspect of ensuring the maximum validity, reliability and practicability of measuring instruments. In case of S.B.A., however, equally important is to make assessment continuous, comprehensive ad cooperative and use the observed outcomes, end-products, results and students' performance to get feed back for improving instructional strategies to get feedback on students' weakness in learning and adapt teaching learning strategies. Purpose is how best to utilize analysis of students' performance to improve teaching, learning and testing processes. Resource material can also be utilized and dynamic interaction can also be generated among various components of assessment. It can also be used for validating and improving assessment objectives, teaching learning strategies and assessment tools. Emphasis of S.B.A. is therefore, extended to improving pedagogical value of measurement.

Thus if teachers become thoroughly conversant with the need for improving pedagogical value of measurement it is expected that they will be able to develop the following competencies:

- (i) Differentiate between the intended and the observed outcomes of teaching learning process.
- (ii) Determine the extent of congruence as well as discrepancy between the intended and the observed outcomes.
- (iii) Diagnose the content area, which demand more attention of teachers for improving students' achievement.

(iv) Identify the assessment objectives on which students' performance is not satisfactory or very poor and may require attention of curriculum experts to judge the validity of such assessment objectives, which might have to be reviewed at a particular level.

(v) Analyse further performance of students on each objective in terms of competencies tested and identify competencies under different objectives on which students' performance is not satisfactory. This forms the basis for remedial teaching to develop such competencies by adapting instructional strategies.

(vi) Analyse students' performance in terms of intended learning outcomes which can be used for improving school inputs or resources, as well as for improving social learning milieu of the school in general to promote better instructional impact on pupils' learning.

(b) ***Setting, Maintaining and Comparing Inter-school Standards***

It is usually the examining agency that sets standard in the form of prescribing syllabus in a given subject and curriculum objectives stated in the syllabus. However, in a given subject intended or stated instructional objectives are better validated through learning experiences provided by the teachers in the class. To what extent good teachers and good learners through good teaching learning strategies were able to achieve the desired, intended or stated objectives, reflect the desirability or otherwise of the standard set in the form of performance indicators. Therefore, relevance of performative set is a function of good testing assuming that mode and technique of evaluation used were valid and reliable i.e. their measurement value as acceptable.

Maintenance of performance standards again demands continuance of good teaching, learning and testing practices by teachers alone who can ensure achievement of attainment targets with the active involvement of learners in various competency based teaching and testing practices besides using well developed question banks for summative evaluation from time to time. This can provide evidence about how well the intended standards are being maintained in terms of intended learning outcomes or prescribed performance indicators. For comparison of inter-school standard of students' performance it is necessary to find out how well students from different institutions in a given state, compare in their performance. It is one of the tasks to set performance standard at state level where some common examination by a board or some other agency. It would also provide good opportunity with the help of teachers, students and examiners and moderated by subject and evaluation experts. This would even ensure inter-school cooperative ventures for improving school based assessment system. If teachers are convinced and start practicing suggestions given above they would be able to to undertake the following tasks:

(i) Set performance standards in terms of instructional objectives and state these in terms of intended competencies.
(ii) Plan, organize and provide efficiently the learning experiences which are relevant to the development of intended competencies.
(iii) Construct and use assessment tools and other devices which are valid to test the developed competencies.
(iv) Select the relevant content elements to develop the intended learning competencies, supposed to be developed.
(v) Maintain desired performance standard by using the same number of higher order questions i.e. based on higher order abilities in testing.
(vi) Identify such areas and instructional objectives in which students' performance is not upto-desired level and reteach using improved instructional strategies.
(vii) Assign students the task of developing higher order questions testing higher order competencies after a particular unit has been taught or learnt by students. This would help them to relearn and improve learning.
(viii) Compare inter-school performance standard of students by adopting cooperative testing programme

once or twice a year and get feed back through analysis of students' performance from different schools.

(ix) Develop in collaboration with other schools, the project on question banking involving both students and teachers of participating schools and utilise the same for summative testing for making comparison as and when required. This can be an on going project.

(x) Undertake in collaboration with some evaluation experts a comparative study of the annual question papers in different subjects, of different schools to study the quality of questions testing higher order competencies, coverage of assessment objectives tested and mode of marking and grading adopted to get feedback for making further improvements.

4.6 Ensuring Equity and Excellence in Testing

(a) *Conceptualization of Equity and Excellence*

In a good system of S.B.A. competency based assessment is the basic component and focal point of assessment. In fact it connotes both quality and equality of learning. It becomes the basis of both norm referenced and criterion referenced testing. It provides the basis for conceptualization of equity and excellence in terms of competencies, which are essential for all students for mastery of concepts and basic skills and are regarded as *Essential Learning Competencies* (ELC) to be mastered by one and all. It is theses ELC's against which mastery and non-mastery can be judged. The other competencies are called *Desirable Learning Competencies* (DLC), which are supposed to be developed by all bright students. These are higher order competencies used for testing excellence i.e., higher order competencies. In fact competency based assessment forms the foundation stone of S.B.A. All these competencies are arranged in hierarchical order on a continuum and depending upon the level and intended outcomes in a subject a line is drawn to bifurcate the ELCS and DLCs. This model of ELC and DLC developed by the author during his tenure as advisor in Mauritius is now operative in C.P.E. examination where passing by all on ELCs (Part I) is compulsory whereas testing of DLCs (part II) cater to all those students who can show excellence by attempting at various levels thereby providing for both equity and excellence.

If teachers are convinced of the need for such a conceptualization of competency based testing it is expected that they will be able to develop the following competencies:

(i) Understand the role of competency based teaching and testing in S.B.A. to achieve the intended learning outcomes.
(ii) Differentiate between the essential and desirable learning competencies in terms of equity and excellence in teaching and learning.
(iii) Illustrate with examples how competency based testing takes care of equity and equality of learning.
(iv) Construct norm-referenced and criterion referenced tests to test the intended learning competencies.
(v) Explain the underlying basis of using ELCs as essential learning outcomes in case of mastery testing of basic concepts and basic skills.
(vi) Interpret students' performance in terms of ELCs and DLCs to diagnose adequacies and inadequacies of learning competencies for adapting or improving instructional inputs.
(vii) Suggest reasons as to why DLCs are used in a good evaluation system.
(viii) Predict impact on students' achievement if DLCs are not included in a good system of assessment.

To sum up

In contrast to external examinations where focus of measuring students achievement is on grading and certification focus of school based assessment has to be made continuous, comprehensive and cooperative assessment with a view to improving students' achievement and instructional impact. Quality of learning and equality of learning are the basis for assessing related competencies. Competency based teaching vis-à-vis testing is indeed the focal point of reform. In order to make assessment system equitable essential learning competencies as well as desirable learning competencies for catering to both equity and excellence in learning. Need for arranging competencies in hierarchical order on a continuum is necessary, ranging from simple to the most complex and bifurcating them into essential and desirable competencies. Use of essential learning competencies for mastery testing of basic concepts is necessary for equity in testing, while testing of desirable competencies cater to excellence in testing and to differentiate among brighter section of students. Using analysis of students' performance on both types of learning competencies provides good feedback to teachers to improve instructional practices to develop those poorly developed those poorly developed competencies, besides predicting the effect of using higher order competencies in teaching and testing, on students' learning. Cognizance of instructional objectives in terms of learning competencies and using them, as basis of teaching, learning and testing is indeed the focal point of reforming the school based instruction and assessment system.

5

Key Concepts Underlying School Based Assessment

Once we understand the philosophy underlying S.B.A. and its objectives we can go ahead for development of a growth oriented model of S.B.A. To appreciate the paradigm of such a model we have to identify the key concepts which form the basis and reflect the focal points of a successful system of school based assessment. A brief description of the key concepts is given below:

5.1 Public Acceptability of the Scheme

Following criteria are relevant for decision-making:

(a) Philosophy vis-à-vis objectives of S.B.A. should be in *accordance* with educational objectives at the national level. There should not be any disagreement with national concerns.

(b) Assessment scheme should be *in conformity* with examination process used for certification of students' achievement by the examination board or examination agency in which school is located. However, S.B.A. processes need not be limited to that.

(c) Scheme of S.B.A. should be *acceptable* to all the stakeholders of reform. Therefore, public in general and professionals including teachers, in particular, must be willing to accept the scheme.

(d) The scheme must be professionally *credible* in terms of:

   (i) assessment objectives of the prescribed course of study.

(ii) holistic assessment of the learner's total development.
(iii) measurement and pedagogical value of testing.

(e) Scheme must be administratibly feasible in terms of its *practicability* in school situation or its learning environments.
(f) It should be economically viable and *cost effective* to implement.

5.2 Continuity and Comprehensiveness of Assessment

(a) *Continuity of Assessment*

This is the most significant and indispensable key component, which cannot be ensured without internal assessment in schools. The teacher who teaches his students can alone undertake learners' assessment continually. Continuity of assessment is necessary to get regular feedback about students' learning as well as instructional impact, which in turn provides the basis for improving students' performance and instructional strategies. Measures like the following, if adopted, can help to ensure continuity of assessment:

(i) Making assessment an *integral part* of teaching by using questions or questioning for readiness testing at pre-instructional stage, for developing the lesson at instructional stage and for reinforcement of learning at post-instructional stage.
(ii) Regular *formative testing* like unit testing provides evidence on inadequacies of students' learning on the basis of which instructional strategies are adopted.
(iii) *Diagnostic testing* becomes integral part of continuous formative testing to identify hard spots of learning on the basis of which remedial teaching can be undertaken to improve students' performance.
(iv) Oral *questioning* during sectional recapitulation while teaching or at the end of a unit of teaching is another mode of continuity of assessment.
(v) Regular use of the school or home *assignments* based on

stated intended learning outcomes of the teaching unit followed by analysis of their adequacies and inadequacies serves good basis of continuous assessment.

(b) *Comprehensiveness of Assessment*

This is a major key concept of S.B.A., which cannot be taken care of, in external assessment. In our educational system we always emphasise total development of learners that envisages holistic assessment of learners', which is possible only through S.B.A. To put it into practice measures like the following can be taken:

(i) Comprehensiveness refers to testing students on all assessment objectives of a subject, which includes both cognitive as well as non-cognitive learning outcomes, possible only through S.B.A.

(ii) Testing of all learning competencies included under different instructional objectives supposed to be developed.

(iii) Use of various modes of assessment like rational, formative and summative at different stages of instruction.

(iv) Use of wide and varied tools and techniques of assessment to collect information about students' achievement on both scholastic and co-scholastic aspects of development.

(v) Involving different personnel like students themselves, peers, class teachers, co-class teachers and even evaluation experts whenever available, to assess students at different stages or occasions depending upon the aspects, activity, and intended outcome being tested.

5.3 Developmental, Standard Setting and Attainment Targeted

(a) *Developmental and Improvement Oriented*

Focus of S.B.A. is not only on measurement value of assessment but also on pedagogical value of assessment. Whatever, the quality of measuring instruments or devices be in terms of evidences collected, unless it is used for improving students' performance and instructional effectiveness its use remains limited to grading and certification of students as in external examination. Since ultimate objective of assessment is to prepare students for their total development a good system of S.B.A. must ensure this by taking steps like the following:

(i) To remain cognizant of the fact that teachers' assessment is to be used for further development of the learners for wholistic development and that requires wholistic assessment possible through S.B.A. system.

(ii) Wholistic assessment of holistic development of learners should be in terms of intended learning competencies, which should include both essential and desirable competencies stated in curriculum objectives.

(iii) Basis of assessment may be criterion referenced testing at the elementary stage where mastery of basic concepts and skills is aimed at. Focus of S.B.A. being on intended criteria i.e. learning outcomes, which in fact reflect the success indicators.

(iv) Use of diagnostic testing followed by instructional correctives and adaptive teaching learning strategies for improving students' performance

(v) Focal points for development and improvement of learners' performance are, self-learning, self-assessment and self-improvement in terms of students' previous performance in views of success indicators reflected in assessment objectives stated in S.B.A. system.

(b) ***Democratic Illuminative Mode of Assessment***

In contrast to public examinations where decision taking is generally autocratic or bureaucratic a good S.B.A. system envisages democratic approach to take decision. All those who are affected by the assessment system or take part in teaching, learning and testing activities are to be involved in taking decisions about the mode of assessment and other related processes. How does the programme work is influenced by various school situations. Illuminative evaluation is based on social anthropological paradigm where cooperative participative role is of concern. It is based on appraisal of complex interaction of various parameters having bearing on pupils' learning. To make S.B.A. more democratic and illuminative, measures like the following can be taken:

(i) Involving different stakeholders in decision-making processes concerned with assessment system in the school.
(ii) Involving various participants and observers in different modes of and activities undertaken for assessment purpose.
(iii) Involving students in examination processes to make assessment more flexible, participatory and stress free.
(iv) Using consensus and descriptive judgments for evaluating students, instructional system and school's learning environments are two central concepts for illuminative evaluation, which improve students' learning and, therefore, should be taken care of.
(v) Undertaking participative cooperative process of assessment, which demands intra-class, inter-class, inter-school and inter-personal involvement in various assessment processes reflecting humanistic evaluation.
(vi) Description and interpretation rather than measurement and prediction are the concerns of this democratic illuminative evaluation.

(c) *Standard Setting and Attainment Targeting*

Since instructional system and learning milieu vary from school to school standard setting would also vary from school to school as also within the same school from time to time depending upon the intake of the students and instructional effectiveness in each school. Similarly time targeting for various intended learning outcomes would vary depending upon students' performance from time to time in different subject areas Moreover, use of objective based testing and development of question banks and their use in assessment can also go a long way in setting standards in a given subject. Measures like following can be taken advantage of, to achieve the intended goal:

(i) Setting of performance standards in a particular subject or subject area can be reflected by developing appropriate instructional objectives in terms of intended learning outcomes.

(ii) Depending upon the intended learning outcomes learning competencies implied in different objectives can be used to reflect intended performance standard. The more the higher order competencies are developed and used in testing the better the performance standard we can expect.

(iii) Keeping in view the class performance from time to time through formative unit testing more appropriate standard can be set in terms of intended learning outcomes through improved instructional strategies.

(iv) Using criterion-referenced approach in testing rather than norm-referenced can better ensure the intended learning outcomes in terms of mastery learning. Of course expected 80 per cent or above may not be possible during earlier stages when we have to target at 60 per cent or so.

(v) Attainment targets can be fixed more realistically keeping in view the quality of students' intake in a school e.g. rural Government school and an urban public school. In fact differential attainment targets would be necessary in case of heterogeneous classes while in homogeneous classes same attainment targets would be possible.

(vi) In actual practice flexible time frame in time targeting would be necessary for bright, average and below average students in case of classes, which have heterogeneous intake of students for admission.

5.4 Quality of Measurement Tools and Techniques

(a) *Tools and Techniques*

Quality is the usual expectation of a good measuring device or instrument of evaluation, whether it is S.B.A. system or a public examination. All evidences collected through assessment tools and techniques become the basis for forming judgments on students' performance followed by taking decisions about students' performance. Therefore, in a good system of S.B.A. it is expected that whatever the mode or technique of assessment is used it must yield evidence which is highly valid, reliable and usable. Following measures can help the teachers to ensure quality of their measurement devices and instruments of evaluation:

(i) Since in S.B.A. teacher who teaches also tests his students and therefore, he is the best judge as he alone knows what and how well he has taught and that ensures *content validity.*

(ii) School teacher teaching a subject alone knows well what was the purpose of teaching a particular topic or unit at different times in terms of instructional objectives related to different units which ensures *curricular validity* of assessment tool or device.

(iii) Consensus of different professionals for rational analysis and sampling of content for assessment ensures *sampling validity.*

(iv) Continuity of assessment, using consensus of opinion in different situations, different modes of assessment and possibility of using much greater number of questions in continuous assessment would ensure improved reliability.

(v) Cooperative development of question banks and their use in testing also leads to better validity and reliability.

(vi) Inter school cooperative testing and question banking lead to better comparison of inter-school students' performance and ensures better usability of assessment tools.

5.5 Adaptability and Flexibility in Assessment

One favourable feature of S.B.A. is its amenability to the desired changes whenever needed for making it workable in terms of intended outcomes. In a way there is a lot of flexibility in using various teaching, learning and testing strategies which can be adapted in view of the evidences gathered through formative evaluation and make it more valid, reliable and usable. Idea is to adapt various assessment practices and make them school specific. Measures like the following are relevant in this context:

(i) Adaptability in terms of weightages to different instructional objectives as well as the learning competencies implied in these objectives.

(ii) Adaptability in terms of time targeting for assessment of various units and terms in view of coverage of syllabus by teachers at a particular time.

(iii) Flexibility in terms of time frame, scheduling and conduct of examination under S.B.A. thereby making it school specific.

(iv) Allowing reasonable flexibility in timing of scheduling tests for allowing students to appear at different times. e.g. if some of them are not ready for final examination or they want to appear after some intervals for improved performance.

(v) Depending upon the students' intake instructional and other academic inputs like staff and financial resources some assessment practices in S.B.A. may be modified, adapted or discarded to suit the learning environments of the school.

5.6 Meaningful Reporting of Students' Performance

In spite of gathering valid and reliable evidence through testing or non-testing techniques of assessment in terms of stated intended learning outcomes in a subject or a unit of assessment if reporting to students, parents or school authorities is not meaningful in terms of learners' own progress, intended performance criteria and norm group to which he belongs it may lead to unwarranted decisions about students' inadequacies and instructional impact. Therefore, for proper judgementing and right decision taking to improve students' learning, instructional strategies and instructional practicing teachers can take measures like the following:

(i) Reporting of students' performance in relation to some norm-group to which a student belongs; that serves as a referent for making judgment. Purpose is to know as to what extent an individual's performance differs from that of the group he belongs to e.g. class, school board examination results etc.

(ii) Reporting can be criterion—referenced when individual's performance is judged in terms of predetermined, specified and acceptable criteria stated in the form of intended instructional outcomes. Its use at elementary stage is significant where mastery of basic concepts and skills is essential.

(iii) Reporting in terms of individual himself, here referent is individual himself, not the criterion behaviour, not the norm group. Self-referenced reporting in terms of his performance at two different times or instructional objective or his rank in the class which reflects his self-improvement and rate of progress.

5.7 Accountability of Practioners

(a) It needs no evidence to support that making practioners of S.B.A. accountable for impact of their instructional effects, proper guidance and administrative facilities, that are reflected in the form of students' performance in various areas of assessment. Comparison of results with previous years or other schools, quality of assessment tools used and such other indicators of success reflected in self-evaluation,. Accountability criteria like the following may be used for judging the effort and efficiency of the practioners of school based system of assessment:

(i) In case of practicing teachers accountability criteria may be in terms of students' performance in annual or public examination as compared to previous years; other schools and board examination results.

(ii) Quality of measuring instrument used for assessment of students.

(iii) Extent of assessment of holistic development as revealed in students' performance on scholastic and co-scholastic aspects.

(iv) Self-improvement as reflected in improvement of ones' qualifications, extra-reading, contribution to journals, action research, etc.

(b) In case of principals or heads of institutions accountability criteria may be in terms of:

(i) better students' intake, facilities and academic resources ensured.

(ii) learning environments favourable for better teaching and learning ensured.

(iii) academic guidance like counseling and guidance services, in service training of teachers, good library, seminars etc, provided.

(iv) School self-evaluation conducted to find out the problems and issues that require attention for improving social learning milieu of the school.

(c) In case of educational administrators or directorate of education in each state accountability criteria like the following may be useful for effective implementation of S.B.A. system:

(i) The extent of facilities provided and utilized by schools.

(ii) Extent of academic resources provided in the form of organizing seminars, training of principals, teachers and supervisors to update their knowledge.

(iii) To what extent inspecting officers were able to judge teachers' efficiency and promote instructional efficiency?

(iv) What incentives or disincentives were provided to motivate the parishioners for better teaching and supervision?

5.8 Cost Effectiveness and Time Targetted Implementation

Efficiency and effectiveness of S.B.A. system has to be judged in terms of time targettedness, resource utilization and cost effectiveness. It is possible that a good system, of S.B.A. conforms to all the above-mentioned criteria in implementing the scheme but it has proved to be too expensive to meet the available financial resources. May be that resources available are not properly utilized and intended time targets for various programmes and activities could not be adhered to. Therefore; for making the scheme of S.B.A. cost effective in terms of utilization of available resources and time targets, measures like the following are considered relevant and necessary:

(i) Wherever possible involve local educated community, others schools and educational agencies for taking academic help in carrying out some projects like question banking, organizing lectures, discussions etc.

(ii) Proper utilization of academic resources for maximum output

(iii) Economical use of financial resources for organizing assessment programmes related to formative and summative testing

(iv) Minimizing expenditure on developing non-confidential question banking through cooperative involvement of students of intra and inter-schools, consulting previous questions papers of different schools and board examinations and getting it moderated by experts from educational agencies through directorate of education.

(v) Utilizing research support gathered through evaluation of different programmes organized from time to improve the existing teaching learning and testing practices.

(vi) Undertaking annual school self-evaluation to find out how best the expenses incurred were utilized to improve learning environments of the school.

To Sum up

The key concepts underlying a good system of school based assessment highlight the focal points or intended criteria, which must be considered essential for learners' total development vis-à-vis holistic assessment of students in a school. Depending on the availability of academic inputs financial resources and the administrative support, system of internal assessment in a school can be improved, updated and made workable in accordance with the desired requirements. A good school based assessment demands continuity in assessment, comprehensiveness of assessment, improvement focused, democratic, illuminative, time targeted and standard setting, quality assurance of measuring device, flexible and adaptable, accountability of the practioners, meaningful reporting of performance, time targeted implementation and cost effectiveness. Above all it should be publically acceptable and stakeholders of reform should be involved as participant observers in various decisions making processes. For improving the social learning milieu of the institution undertaking annual school self-evaluation provides good basis for further improvement of the teaching learning strategies as well as the system of school-based assessment. For further improvement and judging the validity of the basic tenets discussed here let us make a brief over view of the international scenario of school-based assessment described in the next chapter.

6

School Based Assessment: International Scenario

Measurement of efficiency and effectiveness of educational practices is no longer a modern phenomenon. In fact measurement and evaluation has emerged as a special field of education with its own theorists and practioners. Evaluation has become necessary to form judgments on intended outcomes, teaching learning strategies used, impact of programmes undertaken, students' learning and achievement, cost effectiveness of plans and policies, utilization of resources etc. Evaluation has indeed entered the blood stream of our educational system as a potential tool of decision making and establishing a dynamic equilibrium among the various components of the educational process.

External examinations like our public examinations, which are usually labelled as high stakes examinations, are used by many educational systems for selection purpose. Inspite of that these examinations are challenged, for their trustworthiness in reflecting students' performance because of their limited scope of paper pencil tests which mainly provide evidence on cognitive learning outcomes, leaving out largely the other important learning outcomes like the social and learning skills.

Such high stakes examinations are product oriented and tend to impede learning and gear students towards rote memorization rather the deep learning through authentic tasks that are possible in school based assessments. It stifles creativity in some students (Hong Kong report—2003) depress students' initiative, assertiveness and innovations that should be exhibited in their thinking process (Chinese scholar Cheng Fung ping (2002)). Students become robots and get no opportunity for development of other aspects like critical thinking and problem solving. Berry (2005) of Hong Kong institute of Education says, "assessment can serve broader purpose than simply measuring students' achievement and can be treated as a catalyst to learning". School based assessment can reduce the risk inherent in public examinations. Emphasis on school based assessment is not a new idea as many examination bodies like U.K. and Australia have adopted it for the last more than 20 years or so. Internationally, there is a shift in the role of assessing students' achievement for blending of evidences from both sources. The S.B.A. processes and assessment strategies differ in different countries. Portfolios, projects, orals, observations, practical work, surveys etc, are used in internal assessment. Self-assessment, anecdotal records, diagnostic surveys and criterion referenced judgments are also used in many countries. By and large more and more emphasis on school based assessment is now being given because of its inherent potentiality to make pupils' assessment wholistic, diagnostic, flexible and participatory. Purpose is to make it meaningful for reporting, attainment targeted, standard setting, improving students' achievements and instructional effectiveness as well as learning environments of the institution. Establishing dynamic equilibrium among the various components of the teaching learning process is indeed another focal point of reforming school based assessment system.

Following emergent trends are reflected in international scenario:

6.1 Towards Democratic Evaluation

(a) Evaluation role in traditional fact value dichotomy is still to be conceptualized,. Some evaluators defend objectivity by claiming their approaches as value neutral. Others take more radical view and consider value judgment as an indispensable privilege of the evaluator to give meaning to the fact finding mission of the evaluators. Like-wise controversy of qualitative versus quantitative techniques of evaluation is still hot.

(b) Quantitative techniques, which at one time were considered the sine-qua-non of modern social service because of the objectivity of evidence that accrue from their use, are now assailed by advocates of qualitative approach that consider subjective opinion and data collected from participant observers equally significant to form judgment as emphasized by Parlet and Hamiliton in illuminative evaluation. (1977)

(c) Another move is to encourage the non-evaluators to participate in evaluation process, thereby, making evaluation a more democratic process though it will face an uphill struggle against evaluation which is usually conceived purely as a technical process.

(d) Involvement of students in evaluation is another move for their role in self-assessment in New South Wales. While discussing the essential features of an advanced level mathematics syllabus, Afzal Ahmad and William Honor emphasized the need for students to evaluate their own progress to demonstrate their own achievement in terms of knowledge, technical mastery, research and organizational skills, communication skills and application of mathematical insight. For students' involvement in their own mathematical development evaluation dialogue sheet is used regularly by teachers and students besides using peer evaluation to develop students' self-evaluation skills.

(e) John Bennett's paper (1993) on distinctive courses devised for students who complete HSC at the highest level point out this need for non-traditional form of assessment for the nine distinctive courses began in 1992; for assessment in different courses components like written assignment, written examination, viva, orals, research report and project are used with different weightages besides residential seminars, individual research etc. Marks are to be scaled by the board of studies and pupils' results are accumulated during the year.

6.2 Towards Competency Based Attainment Targeting

(a) *"Learning Competencies for All"*

Developed by the Mauritius Examination Syndicate (MES) as a sequel to the publication of the Master Plan of Education (1992) forms the basic philosophy of competency based testing in redesigning the Certificate of Primary Education (CPE) Examination and is the basic document for reform in CPE as well as school based assessment (SBA). The document (1993) describes the philosophy of the project, its rationale and the nature of Essential and Desirable Learning Competencies (ELCs and DLCs) which formed the basis of the new pattern of 1994 CPE examination papers. Introduction of school based assessment was considered essential in order to assess all those competencies also which were not amenable to testing in external examination of CPE.

The author himself, while at MES, proposed the blue print for primary stage with three purposes in view; preparing students for the new pattern of CPE; making assessment an integral part of instruction and getting more valid and reliable evidence about holistic development of the learners. Adaptability, efficiency, learning improvement, participatory mode, accountability, totality and workability were the key concepts identified. Accordingly, a growth oriented model with four frame factors viz. competency, continuity, comprehensiveness and cooperativeness of assessment was developed and presented at the 19th international conference of I.A.E.A. Mode of assessment and tools and techniques are described under scholastic and non-scholastic aspects of development.

(b) *National Attainment Targets*

In Netherland, during the 90's, developments in internal and external assessment in secondary schools highlighted the introduction of core curriculum resulting in the setting of national attainment targets and development of the corresponding nation wide tests to measure these targets in 15 subjects at that time. Levels of targets are left to the schools. Place of school based assessment, mode of assessment, assessment package and external procedures and regulations to guarantee quality of decision process are described with reference data and advisory norms. Challenge to integrate internal and external assessment procedure still remains for professional of CITO

(c) *Assessing against Attainment Targets*

Since the introducing and involvement of national curriculum in 1989 emphasis is on criterion referencing and involvement of teachers in assessment process. Proposed assessment in two parts include Teacher Assessment (TA) and Standard Assessment Tasks (SAT). Collen Robinson in one of his papers gives three reasons; authenticity of assessment, contextual testing and reality testing in favour of school based assessment, besides an amenability to testing of what is not measurable through written tests in favour of school based assessment. National assessment programme in UK requires the pupils to be assessed against all Attainment Targets (AT) by their teachers and some Attainment Targets by SAT at the ages 7, II, 14 and results are combined and reported towards the end of the school year while at 16 external test in GCSE, the grading system which is to be merged with O levels of national curriculum.

(d) *Setting of Attainment Standards*

In Botswana, during the latter part of 1980's, work was going on Nine years basic Education Curriculum and setting the standards for educational attainments which were listed in specific terms. For maintaining standards role of educational curriculum, external examinations, continuous assessment workshops, visits of school inspectors and field education officers are emphasized. Procedure are detailed for comparison of standards. Steps are taken to introduce criterion referenced testing in primary schools with a view to extending it to other levels of learning to pave the way for expressing learner's performance based on well defined domains being measured.

Botswana continues to review school based assessment procedures as well as the external examinations.

6.3 Towards *Holistic Criterion Referenced Assessment*

(a) *Criterion Referenced Performance Criteria*

Assessment of criterion referenced vocational qualifications in the secondary schools by SCOTVEC responsible for development and certification of vocational qualifications in Scotland, refers to some significant features of SCOTVEC system. These include class teacher as assessor, competency based standards, criterion rather the norm referenced performance criteria, no terminal examinations, continuous assessment, remedial action, external moderation and certification by profile of achievement. However, after a number of criticisms leveled at National Certificate New Qualifications called General Scottish Vocational Qualifications are piloted covering the subject of business administration, hospitality, technology and leisure and tourism areas. Qualifications include core skills as well as mandatory and optional units and an additional assessment which takes the form of a project, assignment or case study. Additional assessment is compulsory for all students.

(b) *Incorporating Projects and Practical Work*

In Kenya as a sequel to new education system the Mackey Report (1985) recommended incorporation of projects and practical subjects. Bases of developing instrument of assessment were description of project work, practical work, performance measures, course work, field work and homework. In second cycle of Kenya Certification of Secondary Educational (KCSE), S.B.A. is used in subjects with practical skills which are specified by the specialists in each vocational subject. External assessor assesses and moderates the teachers' school based assessment and his project assessment. Improving the reliability of school based assessment and shift from norm referenced to criterion referenced tests were the challenges for the K.N.E.C.

(c) *Assessment of Psychomotor Outcomes*

Developments in the assessment of practical skills and abilities were summarized by D. Barrett of University of Cambridge Local Examinations (UCLES) and evaluated some of the current instruments of assessment used by UCLES and other examining boards. Detailed analysis was made of the advantages and disadvantages of practical written papers providing a comparative view of validity and reliability of each type of assessment. Course work assessment is moderated by course work moderator. The scheme criterion referenced based on four skills areas, namely; (a) handling apparatus (b) making and recording observations and (c) concluding and moderating. Moderated assessment by 'best fit' matching against performance criteria proved to be a viable technique

(d) *Assessment of Affective Outcomes*

A survey of Scotish teachers indicated their preferences for inclusion of assessment of affective development of pupils as proposed by Hunn report and supported by parents' belief. Three criteria for fairness of assessment described by Dockrel were (a) assessment of a typical; not unusual behaviour; (b) consistency in assessment by different teachers of the same pupil and (c) and comparability of assessment of different pupils by a single teacher. Author recommended inclusion of structured report and provision for open ended record, a profile or a reference. Some studies on traits carried on indicates preferences for traits like confidence, originality, dependability, attentiveness, perseverance etc. of course varying from subject to subject. Assessment of pupils' personal qualities have long term consequences for pupils and for pastoral system and not just for reporting. This area offers very big challenge for the evaluators to identify, relate and distill over the crucial indices of affective learning.

6.4 Ensuring Inter-School Comparability of Learners' Assessment

(a) It does not require any evidence to prove that in institution based assessment subjective judgements of teachers sometimes lead to an unexpected variation in marking. It may be due to the leniency error or severity error of measurement of the examiners or sometimes due to the unintended variation in intended responses. Since school based assessment is now being considered equally important specially in the context of holistic assessment it is essential that we have to find ways and means to ensure that teachers' assessment, both inter-school and intra-school is comparable for proper judgementing of students' performance. Different practices are prevailing in different countries.

(b) In Senior Secondary Assessment Board of South Australia (SSABSA) Coleman described different modes for ensuring comparability of school assessment, through visitation, moderation and statistical moderation. Non-statistical moderation procedures used in SSABSA include:
   (i) Moderation of teachers' programme and assessment plan against syllabus document.
   (ii) Moderation of teachers' marking standard by inspection.
   (iii) Moderation of final school results for each class by inspection of a sample of students' assessment task.

(c) Under statistical moderation school marks are adjusted against external marks regarded as common standard.

(d) Different patterns of assessment and moderation are observable in different subject areas. This may be:
   - 50% external and 50% statistically moderated school based assessment
   - 50% external and 50% non-statistically moderation
   - 50% external and 30% statistically + 20% non-statistical moderation
   - 100% S.B.A using non-statistical procedures

6.5 Towards Quality Assurance System

(a) "The school down the road" reputed for manipulating marks became the focus of discussion of James Strachan of U.K who gave his experience with the school based and external assessment involving moderation issues. Trend to develop its own quality assurance system by each school with less intervention from central system of moderation is moving to next phase (third) — the national qualifications framework which seeks to make the schools own the system. In the paper he examines a number of credibility issues related to school based assessment like assessment status, school status, adversarial attitudes, sign posting and bias. He perceived four characteristics, namely; effectiveness, ownership, signposting and teachers' feedback for enhancing the viability and success of a moderation system.

(b) *Role of Action Research in Quality Improvement*: Since action research deals with the actual classroom problems it is through action research that we can discover the causes of poor performance of learners and get feedback for improving the existing practices to make S.B.A more valid and reliable. I quote a simple example of author's own experience while working as evaluation officer in Himachal Pradesh during early sixties. One of the 21 action research experiments conducted was to use 5, 10, 15 marks for the same question of open-ended variety. Same question was marked by the same trainee first, allotting 5 marks, then 10 and then 15 marks using the same manuscript. The most reliable score came out to be the one when 15 marks were allotted and the least when 5 marks were allotted. Therefore, many of the similar day-to-day classroom problems related to institution based assessment can be solved through action research, which becomes the basis of quality assurance.

Molapi Sebatane attempted to outline a project undertaken for enhancing the capacities and capabilities of primary school teachers in Lesotho as they relate to S.B.A. It indicated that classroom action research has proved to be useful in providing teachers with proper skills and attitudes to conduct school based assessment. It demonstrated that teachers involved in this research oriented approach become self-confident and resourceful, coming up with innovative and relevant research strategies. Besides that they are willing to go out and seek assistance of and share experience with fellow teachers as well as with parents and the community. Certain steps are taken to introduce this approach in the primary school system and necessary measures adopted to ensure its sustainability. Implementation strategy is intended to become an integral part of the overall teachers' training and quality improvement at primary school level as reflected in the five-year plan of development of the Ministry of Education (1992).

(c) Hong Kong's Target and Target Related Assessment (TTRA) is another example of improving the quality of learning in schools through the setting of the learning targets. Three key components of TTRA curriculum framework viz. the learning targets are organized in hierarchy; into units and modules while assessment and reporting of performance elicited through target related assessment tasks for each of the 4 key stages of schooling. Major innovative idea is task related learning, task being central unit of learning which focuses on integration of tasks. Progress in performance is described through a series of 8 bands of performance from primary-1 to primary-5. Learner performance is monitored, recorded and reported through a profile of performance.

6.6 Towards Mix of Internal and External Assessment

(a) *Dichotomy of Internal and External Assessment*: This dichotomy of assessment looms large even today. The onslaughts of external examinations on curriculum development, teaching learning strategies and teachers' assessment of their wards in schools are being criticized more vehemently than before. Predominance of non-referenced external summative measures lead not only to unfair means and malpractices in many of the developing countries but has also made the examination marks as the sacred cow for ranking, admissions and selection of students for employment besides grading and certification of students. This lead to radical opposition to the highly centralised system (upto 1970) as in Portugal with the advent of democratic set up that brought comprehensive schools. The tilt during radical period demonstrated an over-emphasis on internal assessment which resulted in removal of centrally produced external examinations at national level or their substitution by locally produced examinations, thereby putting total confidence in teachers' summative assessment. Nevertheless, the new system while holding up the principle of school based assessment, has introduced a form of external assessment consisting of standardized testing.

(b) *Combining School Based and External Assessment*: New National Curriculum and the associated programme of national assessment introduced in the state maintained schools in England and Wales, as a consequence of 1988 Education Reform Act, involve all children, aged 7, 11, 14,16. Hallmark of this approach is the combination of informal teacher assessment of children's performance recorded throughout the whole year with the external tests known as standard assessment tasks administered by the teacher during the final term of the school year. Final scores are reported nationally very publicly on a school-by-school basis. National curriculum provides a common framework for teaching with clear objectives for students to achieve, involves successive "level" of achievement, described in criterion-referenced terms that students are expected to reach. This lead to raising of teachers' expectations of students' performance and gap between teachers' assessment and results on Standard Assessment Tasks is narrowing. Combined assessment results are reported to parents at end of school year. Positive impact on school practices is noticeable but demand for a less demanding external assessment, in favour of school based assessment along with a slimmer curriculum appear to be the need of the system in vogue.

(c) A discussion paper "The future of certification in Tasmania" produced by school board in 1984 covered a number of options for assessment of students for the new Tasmania Certificate of Education (TCE). Most of the board members and education community were in favour of a mix of internal and external assessment. Teachers found teachers' assessment often more valid and reliable than external one. Of course problem of comparability between teachers and schools is there. Under Tasmania Certificate of Education internal assessments are accepted by the board subject to schools being satisfactorily involved in the process of moderation.

(d) *Effective Use of Portfolios*: Henery G. Macintosh of U.K raised many issues relating to the use of portfolios in school based assessment, like the following:

- Why do we need to review pupils' progress and achievement?
- Who are the beneficiaries of the review?
- What should be reviewed and who should be involved?
- What kind of evidence to be gathered and how to gather?
- What kind of evidence can we gather which is retainable?
- How to select significant highlights from the range of evidences?
- What is to be done with the evidence to be placed in the portfolio?

(e) *The Indian Scene*: In India some commendable efforts have been made under the aegis of N.C.E.R.T, C.B.S.E, Navodya Vidyalaya Samiti and other boards of school education. In spite of that resultant outcomes are not satisfactory. We need to have national achievement survey, on S.B.A to confirm or disconfirm what is suspected besides developing national framework for setting quality assurance system based on inter-related criteria having more public credibility.

To Conclude

From the foregoing discussion on the place of school based assessment we find different countries having different types of perceptions and related problems and intended outcomes. However, one thing is clear that more and more emphasis Is now being given to the teacher based assessments especially in view of the increasing emphasis on holistic development of learners, assessment of which is not possible in external assessment. But credibility of S.B.A is always doubted for lack of objectivity in teachers' assessment and the problem of comparability of students' performance across the schools besides variations in modes of moderation of marks as well as portfolios of assessment. Trend seems to be towards a mix of internal and external assessment. Still evidences are there in some countries where S.B.A has shown more reliability than external assessment. Unfortunately, even teachers themselves are not fully convinced of their own assessments and decry themselves for certification of their own pupils. How to get managers of reform accept that resulting scores from external examinations is not a true reflection of worth when compared to that of aggregation of scores from S.B.A and external assessment, which are more meaningful. How to make public realize that valid assessment of their wards is well neigh impossible without school based continuous, comprehensive assessment which school teachers can alone undertake. These issues are not easy to undertake. Where do we really fail?

Perhaps we can find the answer partially to make the scheme of S.B.A more workable if institutional self-evaluation is undertaken regularly each year to judge the efficacy of the school learning environments and social milieu in which students work. This would require evaluation of school context or setting in which it is working; input evaluation in terms of students' intake and resources available; efficiency of the teaching learning processes undertaken; effectiveness of the assessment devices and instruments used for holistic assessment of learners and the impact made on the attitudes and interests of the school personnel to promote better social and learning environments in the school. Such an analysis would go a long way to improve teaching, learning and assessment practices. This would also help to develop a good growth oriented model of school-based assessment, which will be more acceptable to stake holders of reform.

(*Note*: Since changes in educational system vis-a-vis evaluation system go on, country-wise scenario of S.B.A also under goes review. International scenario depicted here, reflects views presented at a conference of International Association of Educational Assessment)

7

Conceptual Map of School Based Assessment

We have observed in the last chapter that international scenario on school based assessment by and large focuses on the continuity of assessment, comprehensive wholistic assessment of learners, making assessment more flexible, learner friendly and more democratic by involving students and other stake holders in various processes and decision making processes. Trend towards mixing of external and internal assessment, as also quantitative and qualitative assessment and giving weightages to different modes of assessment varies from one country to another. Different studies conducted in different countries do reveal a number of problems related to acceptability of the scheme by the public in general and stake holders in particular e.g. pedagogical credibility, teachers' readiness, fairness in implementation, generalisibility, measurement value of S.B.A. when compared to high stake public examinations or external examinations, cost effectiveness, increased work load of teachers, ensuring accountability of the practioners of the scheme etc. Never-the-less, once we decide to introduce this scheme we have to develop a good model of S.B.A. system. We should be well acquainted or develop a conceptual map of school based assessment to have an overview of the nature and scope of the types of operations involved and intended nature of process to be undertaken. For developing the model a conceptual map reflecting the following process characteristics are visualized:

7.1 Philosophy and Paradigm of *Assessment*

(a) *Philosophy Underlying*

Details of philosophy of S.B.A. are already discussed under chapter 3. Focus is on making assessment more valid and reliable and using the same for further improvement of learners' achievement and teaching learning strategies. This demands familiarity with the following:

(i) *Context of Indian Education*: This needs cognizance of:

- national policies of education,
- national curriculum framework (2005),
- preference for wholistic assessment,
- more valid judgments, and
- full faith in teachers' assessment.

(ii) *Assessment Objectives*: This needs cognizance of:

- evaluation as integral part of teaching,
- measuring learners' performance efficiently,
- improving teaching learning process,
- cumulative hierarchy of instructional objectives, and
- learning competencies implied in different objectives.

(iii) *Principles of Assessment*: This needs cognizance of:

- better validity of assessment,
- improved reliability of assessment, and
- effective usability or workability

(b) *Paradigm of Assessment*

Paradigm of the intended model reflects the pattern we visualize. It requires understanding of the various assumptions we have to make; the key concepts that underly as well as the major frame factors that form the basis or the foundation on which the major model is developed. Therefore, for developing the paradigm we need to be acquainted with the following:

(i) *Assumption About Intended Outcomes:* This needs cognizance of:

- intended achievement of pupils,
- diagnostic function of assessment,
- quality of measuring tools,
- validity of evidence collected, and
- regular feed back on learning and instruction.

(ii) *Key Concepts of Assessment:* This needs cognizance of:

- totality of assessment,
- adaptability and flexibility,
- democratic participation,
- developmental and growth oriented,
- continuity and criterion referenced,
- validity and reliability of assessment, and
- accountability of practioners.

(iii) *Frame Factor of Intended Model*: This needs cognizance of fundamental basis like:

- competency based assessment,
- continuity of assessment,
- comprehensiveness of assessment,
- cooperative mode of assessment, and
- criterion-referenced testing.

7.2 *Assessment Components* and *Modes of Assessment*

Keeping in view the learners' total development and the need for hollistic assessment it is necessary that teachers undertake different types of activities or projects and use various testing and non-testing techniques of evaluation to gather evidence about pupils' growth on all aspects of development. This relates to the following:

(a) *Assessment of Scholastic Aspects*

This needs taking cognizance of:

- subject wise performance of pupils,

- diagnosing inadequacies in students' achievement, and
- getting feed back on instructional effectiveness.

(i) *Assessment of Co-Scholastic Aspects:* This needs cognizance of:

- assessment of physical development, and
- assessment of personal social qualities.

(b) *Mode of Assessment*

Depending upon the purpose, assessment may be made for self-assessment, for getting feed back about students' learning or it may be for making judgments for certifying pupils' achievement. For gathering evidences about students' performance different tools and techniques are used. Assessment mode can be determined keeping in view the following:

(i) *Purpose of Assessment*: This needs cognizance of:

- assessment of readiness for placement purpose at pre-instructional stage,
- assessment as integral part of teaching for developing the lesson, and
- assessment for reinforcement of learning at post instructional stage.

(ii) *Basis of Assessment*: This needs cognizance of:

- rational evaluation,
- formative evaluation, and
- summative evaluation.

(iii) *Techniques and Tools of Assessment*: This needs cognizance of:

- testing techniques like: written tests, oral tests, performance tests, and
- non-testing techniques like: observation, inquiry, analysis, assignment etc.

7.3 Methodology of Grading, Summarization and Reporting

(a) *Methodology of Grading*

Depending upon the aspects of components of assessment numerical or letter grading can be used and judged in terms of cognitive, affective and psychomotor outcomes. In case of performance measures use of process and product performance becomes the basis of assessment. Methodology of grading and judging pertain to the following:

(i) *Assessment of Cognitive Learning Outcomes*: This needs taking cognizance of:

- self-referenced judgments (previous performance/ rate of progress),
- norm-referenced judgments (class/school/state/ board), and
- criterion-referenced judgments (in terms of intended outcomes).

(ii) *Assessment of Affective Outcomes of Learning*: This needs taking cognizance of:

- assessment of habits (study-health-work habits).
- assessment of attitudes and interests, and
- assessment of personal characteristics.

(iii) *Assessment of Psychomotor Outcomes*: This needs cognizance of:

- assessing physical development,
- assessing process of performance, and
- assessing product of performance.

(b) *Summarization and Meaningful Reporting*

Evidences gathered through various modes of assessment are to be summarized in the form of profiles and then reported to students and parents. Summarizing and reporting should be done in a way that it reflects true picture of learners' performance meaningfully providing information about specific strengths and weakness of students. It includes the following:

(i) *Summarization of Evidences Collected*: This requires development of
- individual profiles to reflect assessment of scholastic attainment,
- assessment of personal social qualities,
- class profiles to reflect scholastic and co-scholastic attainments of students.

(ii) *Meaningful Reporting of Students' Performance*: This requires development of individual and class profiles in terms of:
- scholastic and co-scholastic attainments,
- learners' previous performance i.e. self-referenced,
- class, school, or state level performance i.e. norm-referenced,
- intended learning outcomes i.e. criterion referenced,
- weaknesses and strengths in specific area i.e. diagnostic in nature.

7.4 Managing the School Based Assessment Efficiently

Howsoever, good model we develop, which is pedagogically sound, may not achieve the intended outcomes if we are not able to manage the system well. We have to use appropriate operational strategy to make the system work efficiently in order to achieve the intended outcomes of the project of S.B.A. For efficient management of the scheme teachers are supposed to understand the following basis:

(a) *Operational Strategy of Implementation*

This needs cognizance of:

(i) phasing of implementation strategy,
(ii) using participatory illuminative approach,
(iii) use of criterion-referenced formative testing,

(iv) logistics for minimising subjective assessment,
(v) undertaking programme evaluation for feed back.

(b) *Making the System Work*

This demands cognizance of the need for:

(i) use of common framework or design,
(ii) motivating and empowerment of teachers,
(iii) interschool cooperative testing,
(iv) monitoring and evaluation of the scheme,
(v) providing research and other support services, and
(vi) proper utilization of resources.

(c) *Appraisal and Review of the Scheme*

This is the last process characteristics of the model being proposed. Purpose is to judge the functionality of the scheme, get evidences about the effectiveness of the scheme in terms of impact on stake holders, quality of material produced and improvement of social learning environments of the school. Intended outcomes can be judged in terms of the following:

(i) *Impact on Stake Holders*: This needs cognizance of:

- pupils' achievement reflected,
- teachers' professional growth observed,
- quality of teaching learning material produced, and
- quality of question banks produced and used.

(ii) *Functionality of the Scheme*: This needs cognizance of:

- acceptability by stake holders,
- professional credibility of the scheme, and
- cost effectiveness (economical viability).

(iii) *Review of the Scheme for Further Improvement*: This needs cognizancc of:

- evaluating the observed outcome of S.B.A.,
- problems and issues faced in implementation the scheme,

- impact observed on learning milieu through institutional self-evaluation, and
- views and observations of participant observers like inspectors, parents, principals etc.

Annexure provides diagrametic conceptual map of S.B.A.

To sum up

It may be necessary to point out here that while giving the idea of various concepts that form the basis of the model being proposed, attempt is made to emphasise mainly the focal points having bearing on successful implementation of the model. In fact there are many others related concepts and focal points which are not included. Purpose of this chapter was only to pin point the major concepts that underlie the scheme of school based assessment. In a way purpose was to prepare the readers mentally about the conceptual map on the basis of which they would be able to appreciate better the proposed model being discussed in the next chapter.

Annexure

Diagrammatic Conceptual Map of School Based Assessment

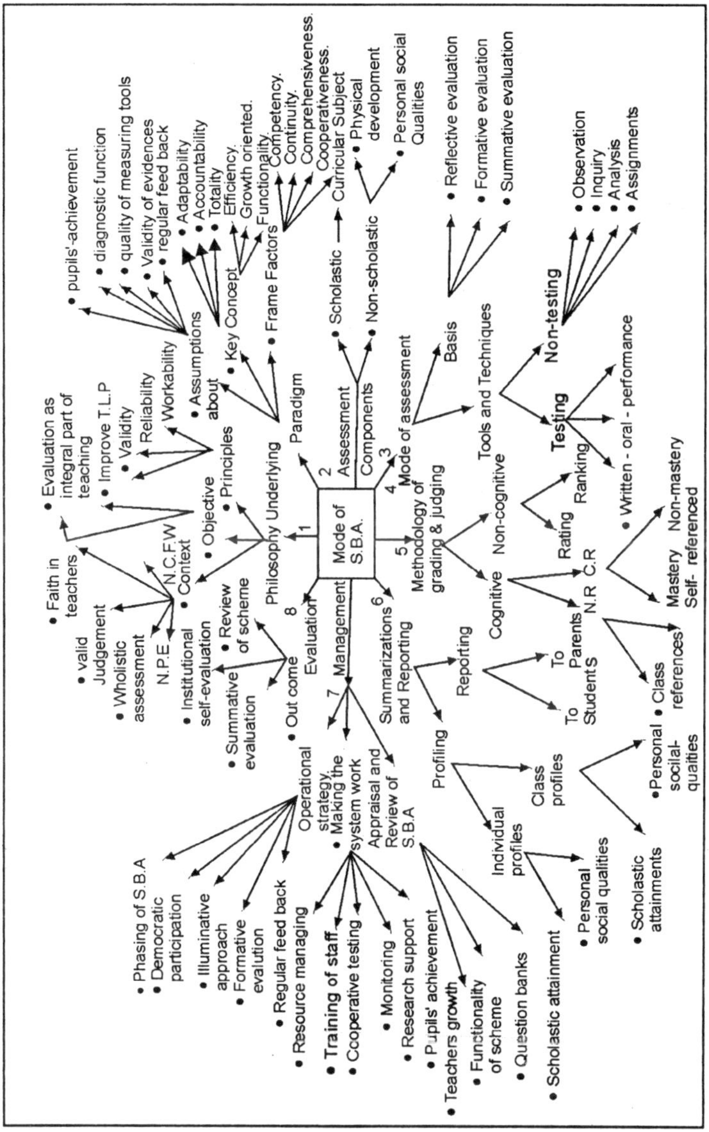

8

Suggested Model of School Based Assessment

8.1 Need for Growth Oriented Model of Assessment

(a) *Developing Pedagogically Sound Model*

In previous chapters we have already made out a case for developing a system of school based assessment which should be acceptable to the stake holders, administratively feasible, legally defensible, pedagogically sound and economically viable. There are different types of models available as reflected in the chapter on international scenario. Though role of S.B.A. is now increasingly appreciated in educational circles because of its scope of wholistic assessment of learners and validity of evidences collected by teachers who teach their wards, yet teacher based assessments are always questioned for subjective, unfair and unreliable grading. In fact question mark on credibility of school based assessments is put because of lack of growth oriented model of S.B.A., boosting of internal assessment marks and lack of expertise in practicing teachers to develop and use good testing and non-testing techniques and tools for assessment of cognitive and more particularly non-cognitive learning outcomes. Though good attempts were made in India during sixties and seventies in Rajasthan, Tamil Nadu, Kerala and other states by N.C.E.R.T., in collaboration with examination boards, yet role of public examinations in selections for institutes of higher learning has relegated S.B.A. system to the background. Somehow a dichotomy in theory and practice of internal assessment still continues. Never-the-less as revealed in the international scenario place of S.B.A.

cannot be ignored because of its potential ability of wholistic assessment which cannot be taken care of in external examinations.

Emerging trends in education for total development of learners necessitates the emphasis on holistic assessment also, which is possible only through school based assessment. But for that, we have to remain cognizant of the key concepts of S.B.A. discussed in details in the chapter 5. Discussion on philosophy and objectives of S.B.A. in earlier chapters lead to the significance of S.B.A. as a total school concept and reflects the impact of the total school environment on learning. It is in this context that we have to develop a growth oriented model which is theoretically tenable and functionally implementable in actual school environments. Before taking up the various frame factors of the model it may be reiterated that we must develop full faith in teachers and their competence to assess their wards efficiently.

(b) *Assumptions made for Proposed Model*

(i) If essential and desirable competencies are made the basis of school based assessment it would focus on demand for equality of learning and excellence in learning, thereby reflecting emphasis on competency based teaching and testing.

(ii) If regular assessment of pupils is made an integral part of teaching learning process it provides needed feed back on learning deficiencies of pupils and basis for remediation besides adapting instructional strategies to improve pupils' achievement.

(iii) If teachers are trained in developing and using criterion referenced tests in terms of intended learning outcomes it would lead to improvement of curricular validity of the evidence collected.

(iv) If holistic assessment of learners is made on both scholastic and co-scholastic aspects it provides more valid data to form sound judgements on pupils' achievements as well as on the impact of instructional strategies adopted.

(v) If cooperative assessment programmes within and across the schools are undertaken it helps the teachers to compare students' performance within and across the schools and provides motivation for pupils to improve their performance standards.

(c) *The Underlying Paradigm*

Related to the above mentioned assumptions we can identify the following attributes that form the basis or the frame factors which indeed provide the foundation of the model to be developed:

(i) Competency based teaching and testing
(ii) Continuous formative assessment of pupils for regular feedback on students' learning and instructional strategies
(iii) Criterion-referenced assessment in terms of intended targeted learning outcomes
(iv) Comprehensive assessment of learners' development and social learning milieu i.e. school's learning environments
(v) Cooperative participatory assessment approach in gathering evidences about pupils 'attainments and taking decisions for further improvement.

8.2 Frame Factors for School Based Assessment

Corresponding to each of the above-mentioned attributes we have five frame factors; namely, *competency based* assessment; *continuity* of assessment; *criterion-referenced* assessment; *comprehensiveness* of assessment and *cooperative participatory* assessment. We can say that they form the basis of the 5-C assessment components (all initialed by the alphabet 'C'. It is this intended integral relationship among these 5-C components which is reflected in the form of tetrahedral model of school based assessment system visualized in the form of a diagrammatical sketch given here-in-after.

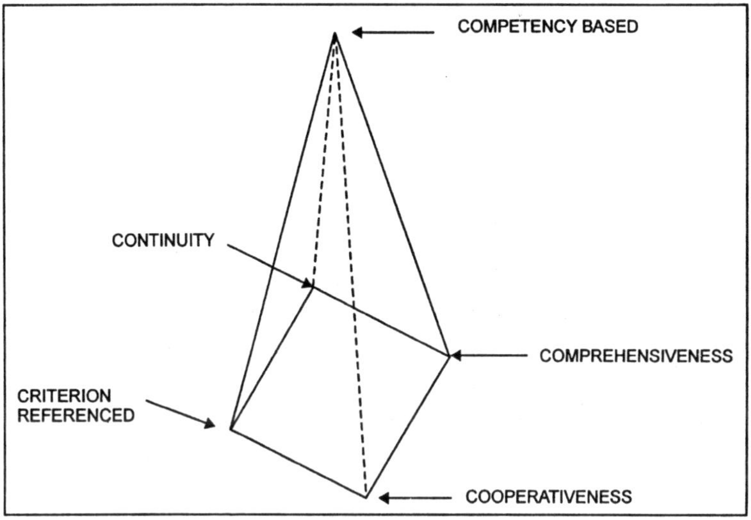

5-C Assessment Components

Implications of each of these components of the model for improving teaching, learning and assessment are described below to highlight the nature, purpose and scope of each with reference to the School Based Assessment (S.B.A.)

(a) *Competency Based Assessment (C-1)*

Since quality refers to both equality of learning (E.L.C.) and excellence in learning (D.L.C.) competency based assessment is the key component representing the apical corner of the model. E.L.Cs are to be acquired by all students (equality of learning) while D.L.Cs cater to brighter section of pupils (excellence in learning). Therefore, while assessing pupils both essential as well as desirable learning competencies are to be made the basis of testing. These competencies can be listed in the hierarchical order of their complexities. More emphasis on higher order competencies (D.L.Cs) in teaching and testing would definitely lead to improvement in instruction and students' learning vis-a-vis performance. Intended learning outcomes when stated in terms of intended competencies to be developed provide needed direction for both teaching and testing. Competency factor, therefore, is the foundation stone of school based assessment and becomes the basis of good instruction and evaluation.

(b) *Continuity of Assessment* (C-2)

Continuity refers to regular, continual, periodic assessments to be used as integral part of teaching-learning process. Competency based unit testing becomes the basis of diagnosing pupils' learning difficulties and applying correctives to improve learners' achievement. Regular feed back of performance about their learning helps them to self-evaluate besides enabling teachers to adapt their teaching strategies thereby improving their quality of instruction. Thus continuity of evaluation leads to better learning, instructional improvement and staff development.

(c) *Criterion-Referenced Measurement* (C-3)

It refers to formulation of unit-wise attainment targets stated in terms of time, speed, content, competencies and acceptable levels of performance. (in contrast to norm-referenced measures where a pupil's performance is judged with reference to his peers, class, school or a state). In case of criterion-referenced measures, pupils' performance is judged in terms of pre-determined criteria or stipulated intended learning outcomes, stated in the form of learning competencies that reflect intended levels of learning. It is against such attainment targets or quality criteria that judgments (criterion-referenced) are made with reference to the learning units which form the basis of periodical testing in S.B.A. However, when purpose of assessment is to grade, rank, select or promote students the norm-referenced deviation judgments are made.

(d) *Comprehensiveness of Assessment* (C-4)

Total development of learners vis-à-vis holistic assessment of pupils' attainments on both scholastic and co-scholastic aspects is essential for collecting valid and reliable evidences about pupils' development. Comprehensive assessment demands utilization of various data sources like, home, school and community involving teachers, principals, peers, parents and community. This requires efficient use of various tools and techniques like testing, observation, analysis, inquiry etc. to get complete picture of pupils' total growth that has taken palce in a particular school context, inputs provided, school processes followed, outcomes accrued and the impact made on school practices.

(e) *Cooperativeness in Assessment (C-5)*

For comprehensive assessment need for participation of school personnel, the parents and the community cannot be under-emphasised to collect data from different sources. Moreover, participatory process of assessment can be extended to school complexes, block and district levels, too. Collaborative inter-school projects like the development of subject-wise question banks, use of common tests for inter-school comparison of pupils' performance, exchange of test material, annual cooperative testing at school complex, block and district levels and organizing seminars and workshops in collaboration with N.C.E.R.T., C.B.S.E., S.C.E.R.T., or D.I.E.Ts would go a long way to make S.B.A. an interactive participatory process to improve quality of instruction, evaluation and other school processes. Annual school-self evaluation by the school can be carried out by the school staff with the help of evaluation experts in terms of school setting, resource inputs, curriculum transactions, learning outcomes and impact on school practices. Further improvement in the quality of teaching learning strategies and assessment procedures and devices can be made in the light of evidences obtained.

The 5-C frame factors of S.B.A. model described above act as foundation stones of the proposed tetrahedral model of S.B.A. that provides direction for improvement of learners' achievement, instructional efficiency, validity of pupils' assessment and the learning environments of schools.

8.3 Adopting *Quality Control Measures*

Once an indigenous pedagogically sound model of S.B.A. is adopted we can apply the following measures to improve upon the existing modes of assessment, quality of tools and techniques, methodology of grading, mode of recording, interpreting and judgmenting about learners, instruction, programmes and outputs, relating to scholastic and co-scholastic aspects of pupils' development.

(a) *Modes of Assessment*

(i) Use of *rational* or logical evaluation for developing an action plan of S.B.A. whose purpose is seeking opinion of experts, views of teachers and parents' reactions to plan and develop assessment procedures besides stock taking of resources, constraints, assess, liabilities and community support. Here focus is on logic, reasoning, opinion and achieving consensus.

(ii) Use of *formative* or developmental evaluation during implementation stage which aims at collecting enroute evidences for feed back to pupils and teachers to enable them to adapt instructional strategies and improve learners' achievement. Mostly it involves criterion-referenced unit testing, oral classroom testing, school assignments and occasional diagnostic testing for remedial teaching, i.e. different modes of formative evaluation. Here focus is on feed back for development and improvement of pupils' achievement.

(iii) *Summative* or judgmental mode involves use of norm-referenced measurement and aims at grading, ranking, classifying, promoting and certification of pupils' attainments as is the case of term, semester or annual tests. Here focus is on judging the outcomes in terms of intended learning outcomes and reviewing the implementation strategies.

All the three modes of assessments are interrelated and when used properly provide useful data that become the basis for quality improvement.

(b) *Aspects of Assessment*

Keeping in view the component of comprehensiveness two

major areas of assessment are the scholastic and the co-scholastic aspects.

(i) *Assessment of Scholastic Aspects:* This would cover areas like the following:

- Subject areas prescribed in the curriculum,
- Participation in the cocurricular activities like debates, quizzes, etc.
- Oral work in languages and the other subjects,
- Practical work, projects work and activities like gardening etc.
- School assignments and home assignments.

(ii) *Assessment of Co-Scholastic Aspects:*This would encompass non-cognitive learning outcomes like the following:

- Learners' physical health or development,
- Learners' health habits, study habits and work habits,
- Learners' interests like scientific, cultural, literary, musical etc.,
- Learners' attitude towards studies, teachers, country, school property etc.,
- Learners' personal, social, spiritual, cultural, universal values.

Within each area of assessment priorities can be worked out depending on the time frame and resources of individual schools.

8.4 Using Relevant Techniques and Tools of Assessment

All the four basic techniques of evaluation i.e. testing, teachers' observations, inquiry and analysis are usable and should be used in different situations to collect relevant information or evidences about learner's growth and development for both cognitive and non-cognitive areas of assessment. Various types of assessment tools are usable for this purpose as described below:

(a) *Assessment of Scholastic Attainment*

(i) *Written Tests*: These include the following types:

- *Readiness Tests*: are to be used for testing pre-requisite learning considered necessary for placement in terms of knowledge and skills to understand the learning unit in hand.
- *Criterion-Referenced Unit Tests*: to be used for testing specified learning outcomes as a par of formative evaluation to identify pupils' strengths and weakness in views of students' mastery of concepts and skills in terms of intended learning outcomes.
- *Term or Semester Tests*: could be used to cover the syllabus in that term or semester. Unlike unit tests purpose of these tests is to grade the students beside giving students the practice of writing longer examinations and preparing them for annual examination.
- *Annual Tests*: are conducted for summative evaluation to form judgments and take decision for grading, promoting and certifying students besides providing feedback to teachers about effectiveness of their instructional effectiveness and enable them to improve teaching strategies.
- *Diagnostic Tests*: are usable when hard spot of learning are identified through unit testing. These hard spots of learning become the basis of developing diagnostic tests. Evidences on such tests indicate the nature of errors the pupils make, on the basis of which remedial teaching and corrective measures are adopted. Such tests help the poor performer to come up to minimum acceptable level. However, need for special orientation of teachers in diagnostic testing is to be realized.

(ii) *Oral Tests*

- Class questioning oral unit tests, oral review session, class quizzes, peer discussion etc. can be utilized for assessment of oral expression, communication skills and other such abilities which are difficult to assess through written tests.

- Nature of oral tests, number of oral tests and timing of oral testing or assessment will be flexible, school specific and teacher specific.

(iii) *Performance on Assignments*: Regular use of school and home assignments have to be made to reinforce what is learnt and develop in students the ability to use what is learnt. Different types of assignments like knowledge assignments, review assignments, reinforcement assignments and transfer assignment can be used depending upon the purpose of assessment. Feedback on these assignments would help teachers to undertake needed correctives to improve students' achievement.

(iv) *Practical Tests/Projects/Activities*: Certain activities like games, sports, gardening, dancing etc. involve different types of psychomotor outcomes of learning. Their assessment can be undertaken to appraise practical skills, communication skills organizational skills, perseverance, work habits and other character building values.

(b) *Assessment of Co-scholastic Aspects*

For assessment of co-scholastic aspects following tools and techniques can be employed by teachers. Of course it is expected that teachers are properly trained in using them efficiently and make meaningful interpretation of data gathered through various techniques and tools of assessment.

(i) *Observation Technique*: It is the most usable and significant technique for assessment of all the co-scholastic aspects like habits, interests, attitudes, values and other personal and social qualities. For validity significant incidents of behaviour are identified and observations are made; properly recorded and cautiously interpreted. *Observation schedule* is the main tool used for making planned, accurate and objective observation. For more reliable observation it is better to have more than one observer. For unbiased and objective observation and dependable evidences observer must be cognizant of:

- What is to be observed?
- What is the purpose of observation?
- When and how many times observation are to be made?
- When and how to record? and
- How cautiously and meaningfully to interpret the evidences?

(ii) *Inquiry Techniques*: There are various modes of inquiring about students' difficulties, their problems, preferences, limitations, relationships, views and many other personal social qualities. Interviews, sociometry, opinion surveys etc. are usable techniques of inquiry, while interviews schedule, sociogram, opinionaire etc. are the corresponding tools applicable to inquiry.

(iii) *Ananlysis Techniques*: This technique refers to analysis of results, opinions, views, content, syllabus, data, evidences etc. For this tools like proforma, check list, rating scale, record card, cumulative record card, graph, progress report etc. can be used.
Analysis of achievement record of learners provides information on attainment of assessment objectives. Analysis of content of a unit helps to delineate the content elements to be learnt. Analysis of test results reveals adequacies and inadequacies in learning vis-vis the instructional effectiveness. Analysis of a diagnostic test helps to identify the cause of poor performance. Analysis of outcomes of pupils' participation in different activities which shows interest of pupils' and so on.

Thus besides written and oral tests and practical exercises or projects we make use of assessment tools like observation schedule, interview schedule, rating scale, check list, sociogram, questionnaire, anecdotal record, pupils' products etc. for assessment of co-scholastic aspects in school based system of assessment.

8.5 Methodology of Grading and Data Processing

Concept of mastery and equality of learning should indeed be the basis of grading at the elementary stage. Testing for mastery of basic concepts through criterion-referenced testing paves the way for improvement of achievement. Though different levels of mastery prevails due to individual differences, the fact remains that given the proper inputs in terms of instructional efficiency, time allowed for learning and regular diagnosis of learning difficulties followed by remedial teaching most of the students would acquire mastery. Thus at the primary stage only 2 point grading, in terms of masters and non-masters, would alone be reasonable and therefore, recommended for classes 1-5.

In case of upper primary classes (middle stage) further dichotomy of mastery and non-mastery states leads to 4 point classification, two under mastery and two under non-mastery i.e. A and B, C and D. In terms of marks the four grades, we have 80 per cent and above as A, 60-79 as B, 40-59 as C and below 40 per cent as D. To avoid teachers' tendency to rate students towards central grade point (C or B) in a commonly used 5 point scale the four point scale is recommended. To begin with even a little lower level of mastery can be stipulated (75-100, 50-74, 35-49, below 35%) for grade A, B, C, D. Focus would however, remain on attaining mastery and remedial teaching to improve students' level of attainment. Therefore, 4 point grading via marking in case of scholastic aspects and direct 4 point grading for co-scholastic aspects is recommended for upper primary classes. At the secondary stage however, it is better to adopt the same grading system in S.B.A. as recommended by the C.B.S.E. or examining agency with which the school is affiliated. The most acceptable pattern of 9 point grading (via marking) on the curve appears to be the most acceptable system of grading on which debate is still going on in India.

8.6 Judgmenting, Decision Taking and Reporting

Three types of judgments can be made serving different purpose. In terms of students' own progress self-referenced judgments can be made to help them to know about their rate of progress through self-evaluation. Criterion-referenced judgments can be made in terms of mastery or criteria of intended learning assessed on the basis of criterion-referenced tests as in unit testing. Feed back on such tests helps to diagnose pupils' learning deficiencies and provides basis for corrective measures besides adapting their teaching learning strategies. The third type of judgements are norm referenced judgements which can be made in case of term and annual examinations where students' performance graded and compared with his peers, class performance and even across the schools at district or block level when common testing is adopted or cooperative testing is undertaken by different schools.

All assessments on different aspect like subject based tests, orals, participation in co-curricular activities, assignments projects, and personal social qualities should never be combined but kept separately for appropriate analysis, feedback and follow up action. Performance in these areas are to be separately recorded and reflected in the form of students' profiles to make it more meaningful and diagnostic for appropriate action. On the basis of students' profiles, depicting performance on the various components of assessments may be developed for comparison with performance of students of different sections and even with students of these schools if need be. Such a reporting system provides a clear picture of students' strengths and weaknesses in specific areas on the basis of which proper decisions can be taken related to improvement of pupils' performance, instructional strategies and learning environments of the school.

To Sum Up

It hardly needs any mention that any model which is proposed for developing good system of school based assessment must conform to the emerging trends in education, and acceptable to the stake holders. Attempt is made in this chapter to suggest a growth oriented model of school based assessment which is theoretically tenable, pedagogically sound and functionally operative, in the Indian context. While discussing the philosophy and objectives of S.B.A. and the key concepts underlying, significance of S.B.A. as a total school concept reflecting the impact of total school environment on pupils' learning five frames factors are identified leading to proposed tetrahedral model. Assumptions underlying the proposed model followed by related attributes and corresponding frame factors lead to the five assessment components of competency, continuity, criterion referenced, cooperativeness and comprehensiveness. Competency factor is regarded as the foundation stone of S.B.A. and becomes the basis of instruction and evaluation.

Once this model is adopted various quality control measures are to be taken to improve the existing position. This includes improvement of modes of assessment with respect to scholastic and co-scholastic aspects of pupils' holistic growth and development using various devices of assessments. Methodology of grading and processing of data is suggested in terms of mastery and equality of learning using criterion-referenced testing. Issue of direct grading and grading via marking and 9 point grading at different stages, elementary and secondary are discussed. For judgementing, decision taking and reporting, place of self-referenced, criterion-referenced and norm-referenced judgements is highlighted besides the role of individual pupil's profiles and class profiles for better comparability of students' performance across the schools.

To summarise, various steps involved in developing school based assessment are given here in after in the annexure.

Inspite of a good theoretical model it may fail unless implementation strategy is relevant and functional; which is dealt in the next chapter.

Annexure

Steps in Developing School Based Assessment

1. *Visualise*: context and background of the school.
2. *Take*: cognizance of the predisposing factors like time, strength, resources.
3. *Acquaint*: yourself with the objectives of the primary stage.
4. *Formulate*: subject—wise objectives in conformity with the stage wise objectives.
5. *Specifity*: subject wise objectives in terms of performance indicators like ELC/DLC
6. *Determine*: priority assessment needs.
7. *Clarify*: the purpose of assessment.
8. *Delineate*: the relevant mode of assessment to be used.
9. *Decide*: the relevant evaluation instrument to be used.
10. *Select*: the relevant evaluation instrument to be used.
11. *Observe*: three basic criteria of measuring instrument for construction
12. *Apply*: relevant tools and techniques for collecting evidences.
13. *Summarise*: evidences into meaningful profiles.
14. *Form*: accurate and appropriate judgements about students' achievements
15. *Take*: appropriate decisions for diagnosis, remedial action and promotion.
16. *Report*: to students, parents and other clientele for timely feedback.
17. *Use*: results, evidences and feedback data for improvement of teaching learning strategies and students' learning.

9

Operational Strategy for Effective Implementation of S.B.A.

In the last chapter a blue print of the growth oriented model of school based assessment was proposed. The 5-c tetrahedral model shown diagrammatically reflected the assessment components which formed the basis of the system of S.B.A. Although attempt is made to develop a theoretically tenable and pedagogically sound model of S.B.A. it would lead to the intended outcomes only if the implementation strategy ensures that the system works efficiently. For this evidences gathered and grading of students on their academic achievement through norm-referenced testing undertaken in different schools should be comparable in terms of performance measures adopted for certification of students' attainments across the schools within a block, district or even a state if S.B.A. is to be moderated by the board conducting the public examination. For minimizing inter-school variance in assessing the students and ensuring parity of grading in different schools steps like the following are relevant:

9.1 Adopting Democratic Mode of Evaluation

(a) *Using Participatory Approach Involving Stake Holders*

Keeping in view the international scenario of democratic mode of evaluation it is necessary that at various stages of S.B.A. all those who have stakes in the outcomes of assessment system, be involved. For gathering comprehensive evidences about pupils' total growth, involvement of all such functionaries from the school, community, department and home who can throw light on various aspects of pupils' growth is necessary. Besides getting collaboration of educational agencies like NCERT, SCERTs, and departments of education etc. it is advisable to pool opinion, views, information, observation and impressions of teachers, principals, pupils, peers, parents, community members and other stake holders making it cooperative, participatory enterprise whereby it is possible to illuminate maximally the aspects covered, competences developed and cherished values imbibed. It will help in making S.B.A. more valid and objective.

(b) *Adopting Common Design of Assessment*

Examining agencies like boards of secondary education in collaboration with central agencies like N.C.E.R.T. should develop and prescribe a common design of S.B.A. for secondary stages. Directorate of Education in collaboration with S.C.E.R.Ts can work out specification of instructional objectives, weightage to different components of assessments, criteria of assessing scholastic and non-scholastic aspects, nature of evidences to be collected, mode of evaluation, usable tools and techniques of assessment, methodology of grading, judgementing, summarizing and reporting. Such common blue print if followed by all schools within the specified area of operation would ensure better comparability of students' performance across the schools.

(c) *Ensuring Impartial and Unbiased Marking*

More subjectivity does not mean curtailing of teachers' freedom in grading of students but refers to ensuring impartial and unbiased marking by teachers for fair, just and objective marking. Since failure of the scheme is usually attributed to teachers' subjective marking and judgementing on pupils' performance, measures like the following, if adopted, would reduce it to the minimum and make teachers' assessment more objective and dependable for making appropriate decisions.

(i) Strict monitoring and evaluation of action tasks in terms of time targets, enroute products and intended learning outcomes.

(ii) Adoption by teachers the same common design and criteria of assessment as provided in the blue print of the scheme allowing flexibility in timing frequency and using tools and techniques of assessment.

(iii) Using well designed and constructed tools of assessment incorporating more short answer and fixed response questions with well constructed marking scheme to ensure maximum scoring objectivity.

(iv) Frequent use of the common tests developed through common test pool developed through interschool collaboration.

(v) Developing and using accountability criteria for judging teachers' efforts, efficiency and effectiveness of instruction.

Purpose of the above mentioned measures is to ensure maximum objectivity, fairness and impartiality in marking and grading, without curtailing much of the teachers' freedom to assess students in their own way.

9.2 Planned Introduction and Follow-up of S.B.A.

No school based assessment is complete unless assessment of co-scholastic aspects is included for ensuring holistic assessment but the fact remains that it requires serious efforts and time to make it practical and subjectivity free. Even in case of assessment of scholastic aspects researches show that a lot of subjectivity prevails in marking even in public examinations what to talk of S.B.A. by teachers. Therefore, school authorities in consultation with its staff and related agencies like D.I.E.Ts, S.C.E.R.Ts, N.C.E.R.T. and Directorates of Education should develop implementation strategy identifying the action tasks at various stages. It is suggested that phasing of reform may be done as under:

(a) *Phasing of Reform*

This refers to:

- Assessment of scholastic aspects to be followed by non-scholastic aspects which require mostly the non-testing techniques of assessment.
- Phasing of the attainment targets at different stages; elementary etc.
- Mode of assessment: testing to be followed by non-testing techniques.
- Frequency or periodicity of assessment according to unit-wise teaching.
- Use of common design be worked out when assessment of non-scholastic aspects are introduced.
- Criteria of assessment, mode of assessment, recording, summarization of evidences, judgementing and reporting should also be similar, across the schools.

For planned introduction of S.B.A. we have to develop implementation strategy which reflects various action tasks at different stages as delineated below:

(i) Planning Stage: This would include

- decision to be taken about phasing of reform
- time targeting and calendar of activities to be followed.
- listing of success indicators in terms of intended outcomes.
- mode of inbuilt evaluation and feed back mechanism.
- cognizance of constraints as availability of resources.
- knowledge of existing system of S.B.A. and its limitations.

(ii) *Preparatory Stage*: This would include tasks like

- study of existing position of school based assessment.

- developing the document on the scheme of intended S.B.A.
- creating suitable machinery for implementation.
- time targeting and formatting of action tasks.
- developing training packages and exemplar material.
- orientation of resource persons supervisors, heads and subject teachers.
- establishing linkages with other educational agencies.

(iii) *Implementation Stage*: At this stage tasks like the following are:

- recurrent training of teachers and other staff.
- introduction of assessment of scholastic aspects (1st Year) followed by inclusion of non-scholastic aspects for assessment.
- supply of exemplar material on testing to schools.
- introduction on institutional banking project on cooperative basis.
- undertaking formative and diagnostic testing.
- development of record cards and record keeping.
- coordinating, monitoring and supervision of activities.
- undertaking studies, investigations and action research.
- appraisal of school processes, outputs, impact and collateral effects.

(iv) *Summative Evaluation Stage*: This would include

- appraisal of students' achievements in terms of cognitive and non-cognitive outcomes of learning.
- appraisal of professional growth and perception.
- appraisal of programme effects, intended and unintended.
- appraisal of learning environments of the school.
- undertaking school self-evaluation in terms of school setting, inputs given, curriculum transactions, outputs and impact on school practices.
- inter-school comparison of students' performance.

(v) *Review and Renewal Stage*: At this stage tasks to be undertaken are:

- close look at observed outcomes, instructional effectiveness, impact on school practices and learning environments of the school.
- revalidation of learning competencies.
- utilization of resources and cost effectiveness.
- effectiveness of implementation strategy in terms of assessment objectives.
- conducting follow up studies and functional research.
- disseminating the findings of summative evaluation to concerned functionaries.
- review and renew the scheme of S.B.A. to make it more efficient and functionally operative.

9.3 Motivating and Empowering the Teachers

(a) *Providing Intrinsic and Extrinsic Motivation*

Since school based assessment is the prerogative of teachers only, it is necessary that they should be depended upon. Faith in their competence and belief in their right to assess their wards are basic premises of S.B.A. Empowering of teachers requires following actions.

(i) Proper motivation at the time of introducing the proposed system of S.B.A. and also during the course of teaching learning process.

(ii) Intrinsic motivation which can be provided by giving them the idea that total assessment is left to them because full faith is reposed in their competence.

(iii) They may also be informed that when pupils are given opportunities for developing affective learning outcomes, they get interested in the subject concerned as it accelerates their cognitive learning.

(iv) Extrinsic motivation can also be provided in the form of awards and special certificates to such teachers whose assessment compares well with the performance of their pupils in public examination in case of assessment on scholastic aspects.

(v) Similar other incentives can also be used which may be school specific and learner specific, to help teachers assess objectively.

(b) *Continual Training and Retraining of Teachers*

For empowering teachers further steps like the following are usable:

(i) Regular training and retraining is indispensable for successful implementation of any system of school based assessment.

(ii) Organizing seminars and workshops to make teachers understand the proposed theoretical model of S.B.A., which provides the needed framework and the 5-C assessment components.

(iii) Provide guidelines for assessment of holistic development, criteria of assessment, modes of assessment and techniques of assessment.

(iv) Arranging participatory discussion on methodology of recording evidences, mode of summarization, profiling and modes of judgmenting.

It is through such orientation programmes that teachers get motivated and empowered to implement the scheme efficiently.

9.4 Logistic for Minimizing Subjectivity in Assessment

Subjectivity in teachers' assessments is the main cause of failure of S.B.A. Besides motivation and empowering of teachers and other administrative measures there are some other pedagogical measures which if taken can reduce subjectivity in marking and grading to the minimum. For example following measures are relevant in this case:

(a) ***Minimising Intra and Inter School Variance in Assessment***

(i) Using various types of incentives for teachers showing unbiased, just, fair and impartial assessment as evidenced by comparable pupils' performance in board's examination and also through other indirect measures like pupils' opinion.

(ii) Using the same common prescribed design and criteria of assessment strictly across the schools

(b) ***Improving the Quality of Assessment Tools***

(i) To make question paper more valid and reliable by increasing the number of objective type and short answer questions.

(ii) Wording of the questions more appropriately, using simple, concise and unambiguous language to make the intended scope of the answer clear and use of directional words appropriate to delineate the scope of intended answer in case of free response questions.

(iii) Developing the marking scheme in details after trying out the same and giving the intended value points with allocation of marks credit-wise. Still better if the marking scheme is discussed in an open session by the examiner.

(iv) It is better if examiners are asked to mark the answer scripts question-wise across the scripts rather than script wise.

(v) Using common test developed through commonly developed question pool in testing.

(vi) Associate multiple raters in marking to reduce subjectivity in marking.

(vii) Reduce the number of essay type questions as far as possible to reduce subjective marking.

9.5 Providing Research and Other *Support Services*

In order to support such a big project as S.B.A. it is essential that provision of different services may be made to support various programmes which help to carry out the project successfully. Following are some support services which are relevant in this context.

(a) *Publicising the Reform being Introduced*

If dissemination of reform outputs is not done regularly it lowers the acceptability of public since they remain ignorant of what exactly is the reform about and what useful impact it could have. Full advantage may, therefore, be taken to publicize the relevance, significance and the likely impact of the reform through mass media, like the news papers, radio, television, news bulletin, booklets etc. and through teachers' conferences.

(b) *Sustainable Factors to Support Reform*

Services like motivation of teachers, reinforcement of innovations, continuous supply of test material to the teachers to construct good test and follow up work are relevant in this context. A brochure on exemplar material in the form of unit test, diagnostic test or on different forms of questions prepared in collaboration with subject and evaluation experts from different educational agencies is useful for guidance of teachers. Encouraging establishment of question banks in schools for improving teaching and testing practices is another sustaining factor to carry out S.B.A. practices more smoothly.

(c) *Establishing Linkages*

When linkages with allied educational agencies like N.C.E.R.T. and N.C.T.E. is not effective it affects sustainability of reform. Close interaction and participation of agencies like panchayats, D.I.E.Ts, S.C.E.R.Ts, teachers' training institutes, neighbouring schools, directorates of education and even non-governmental voluntary agencies will definitely strengthen the academic fibre and administrative support to sustain the on going reform of school based assessment system.

(d) *Provision of Feedback Services*

In built formative evaluation which is an integral part of teaching provides the needed feedback about pupils' learning and other attainments that help the teachers to adapt their instructional strategies and undertake remedial measures. Feeding the teachers with relevant literature in the form of video tapes, handouts, news letters, teachers' meets etc. all help in sustaining the reform. Teachers get demotivated if community support, parent teachers' associations and teachers' association do not provide support. Keeping contact with them by keeping them informed about the progress and outputs of their efforts and appreciating them in such meetings for their role, are all in a way the services that support the reform programme.

(e) *Providing Research Support*

Research support is seldom provided to the ongoing reform since it is time consuming and requires the financial help and technical competence to undertake functional and action research. But funding of such research if incorporated does support the reform and improves the situation. Problems emerging through enroute formative evaluation need empirical evidences before they are incorporated in the system of S.B.A. Depending upon the need and findings following types of researchers can be undertaken:

- (i) Case studies of good and poor schools
- (ii) Follow up studies and impact studies
- (iii) Study of collateral effects of the reforms introduced
- (iv) Analysis of question papers in terms of intended learning outcomes
- (v) Development and use of school based question banks
- (vi) Validation of learning competencies and placement of concepts

Research support helps to improve instructional and implementation strategies besides staff development. Exemplar material, achievement surveys, ready made criterion-referenced tests and recurrent training of teachers provide good services for making S.B.A. a success.

9.6 Proper Monitoring, Evaluation and Supervision

Monitoring refers to direction, supervision, guidance and coordination of action tasks, being carried out to see that they are carried out in accordance with time frame for attainment of pre-determined targets in a manner that the system works efficiently. It has to be done at two levels.

(a) *Monitoring of Reform*

(i) At the school level principal or deputy head acts as a coordinator who would develop the action plan indicating the broad frame work, identifying the action tasks, role of subject teachers, schedule of activities, mode of implementing, time targeting and feed back mechanism. It would reflect on competency based teaching, role of criterion-referenced and norm-referenced testing in unit testing and annual examination, developed cooperatively by school staff. It would also reflect on use of diagnostic tests from time to time followed by remedial teaching. The coordinator of S.B.A. would also develop a formatting chart to monitor the time schedule of various tasks and activities ad mode of summarizing data, profiling and reporting to pupils, parents and teachers themselves.

(ii) Second level of monitoring and coordination would be done at the level of board or the examination agency concerned so that the schools follow the prescribed mode, procedure and mechanism in carrying out the S.B.A. as objectively as possible. It may include tasks like the following:

- Ensuring use of common design, criteria, and assessment procedures
- Training and retraining of teachers and other staff
- Providing technical support to schools for cooperative development of question banks and cooperative inter-school testing

- Helping schools to undertake inter-school programmes of formative and summative evaluation
- Providing exemplar material in the form of competency based test items and other related literature
- Carrying out achievement surveys for judging, comparing and maintaining performance standards

(b) *Appraisal and Review of the Scheme*

How far the scheme has proved to be successful in terms of stated objectives has to be appraised to know the discrepancy between the intended and the observed outcomes. For this whole system and framework of the institution has to be kept in view This can be judged in terms of outcomes, school self-evaluation and success indicators.

(i) *Outcome Evaluation*: This include the following outcomes:

- Pupils' achievement in curricular areas and also non-cognitive development when included in the scheme of S.B.A.
- Teachers' growth and development in terms of professional competence, interest in children, attitude towards profession, values imbibed etc.
- Action tasks and programmes undertaken to achieve the intended objectives stated in the scheme of S.B.A.
- Teaching learning material produced and used during curriculum transaction and assessment.
- Impact on learning and social milieu of the school in terms of creating social climate and learning atmosphere conducive to learning.

(ii) *School Self-Evaluation*: While evaluating the above features it is essential that it is done within the framework of school system. Therefore, teacher evaluation and programme evaluation are all necessary to portray the complete picture of the school besides pupils' evaluation in terms of its own setting, inputs provided, processes undertaken, outputs accrued and the impact made in terms of intended and un-intended effects. Thus exercise of school self-evaluation is necessary to know adequacies and inadequacies of the total school environments which contribute to the total development of the learners. In such an exercise principal, teachers, students, community members and block education officers may be involved. For making the evaluation more valid and reliable some evaluation experts may also be associated to develop the paradigm for assessment.

(iii) *Success Indicators of S.B.A. System*: Keeping in view the philosophy and objectives of S.B.A. following types of indicators can be considered as outcome of effective instruction and efficient assessment system and conducive learning environment of the school.

(a) Reduction in the incidence of failures
(b) Improvement in the performance level of students
(c) Inter-school disparities in students' performance has reduced in schools within the same categories.
(d) Improvement in attainment level on co-scholastic aspects has improved pupils' achievement on scholastic aspects.
(e) Validatation of learning competencies and their proper placement and sequencing for different classes
(f) Improvement in quality of evaluation material used
(g) Observable changes in instructional practices and teachers' attitudes towards pupils, S.B.A. and professional commitment
(h) Positive impact on school learning environment ad social milieu
(i) Workability of the scheme in terms of operational strategy

9.7 Ensuring Autonomy, Transparency and Accountability

Inspite of common design and uniform criteria of assessment schools are quite autonomous in terms of time targetting, frequency of assessment use of tools and techniques to gather evidences and other related tasks. Subjectivity would still continue to prevail with respect to teaching, quality of assessment tools, mode of interpreting and judgmenting. Whims and fancies of administrative staff, unsupportive attitude of parents and community members and lack of incentives for teachers could impact adversely the efficiency of S.B.A. To make all these stake holders of reform responsible for actual outcomes and desired impact on teaching learning practices, it is essential that accountability criteria in the form of clear cut indicators of success be worked out in terms of efforts put in, efficiency in school processes and effectiveness of outputs be worked out with the help of curriculum and evaluation experts and stipulated for practioners of S.B.A.

Unless accountability of each trustee of reform is at stake it is difficult to ensure practioners of reform to deliver the quality goods in time. Teachers have to be told about the criteria or the indicators of effective teaching and testing on the basis of which their performance will be judged. Like wise supervisory staff must also be made cognizant of the time tabling of activities and the time targets for which they would also be made responsible, accountable for timely providing the teachers facilities, financial resources and related services besides development of human resources. Therefore, for carrying out S.B.A. efficiently as per stated objectives of S.B.A. clear cut indicators have to be worked out by experts for all the practioners of reform and prescribed for various functionaries.

To Conclude

Establishing a sound system of S.B.A. is quite demanding and require cooperative planning, continual vigil and replenishment of resources. Reformulation of action tasks, adaptation of implementation strategy, phased introduction of reform and formative evaluation of enroute products for feedback and correctives are necessary steps. Use of participatory approach involving stake holders, adopting common design of assessment for all institutions, minimizing subjectivity in the assessing pupils by fair and just assessment, planned introduction and follow up, phasing of reform, motivating and empowering of teachers, providing research and other support services, proper monitoring and supervision and evaluation of programmes and activities, appraisal and review of the scheme in terms of outcome evaluation, success indicators and school self-evaluation for social and learning milieu of the school, providing intrinsic and extrinsic incentives and to provide needed autonomy, transparency and accountability of all the functionaries involved are imperative factors for effective strategy of implementation of S.B.A. system. Annual review and renewal of the scheme is necessary to make it more valid, reliable and workable which in turn contribute to improve the quality of teaching learning process.

10

Promoting Quality of Education Through School Based Assessment

School based assessment is an integral part of teaching learning process. How best to use S.B.A. for promoting quality of education depends not only on the relevance of SBA but also on criteria of quality school education which act as pre requisites with which teachers have got to be familiarized. The most important is the knowledge of national goals of education so that whatever steps are taken to improve quality of education these must conform to and be in agreement with these goals. Moreover, quality of education has to be reflected in the form of intended outcomes of learning or indicators of quality which would provide direction for developing quality curriculum which is prescribed to delineate further subject wise instructional objectives and curriculum content. For curriculum transaction in classroom, quality instructional material as well as good teaching learning strategies material are necessary. Unless teaching learning material and strategies are relevant and efficiently used it may not lead to intended learning outcomes.

Quality of education is also improved by providing effective learning and social environments for which it becomes essential that learning and social milieu of the school be made favourable. This may require improvement in setting, inputs, processes and outputs of the school. Another significant factor affecting quality of school education is the quality of the assessment system itself used for promoting quality of education. Thus for promoting quality of education school based assessment system should be such which must reflect properly the success indicators to be used as criteria of successful system. Use of sustainable strategy of implementation of SBA, all the three modes of assessment, reflective, formative and summative, as also diagnostic testing followed by remediation, ensuring measurement value of assessment and using assessment as a feedback device to improve teaching learning process are other action tasks relevant for improving the quality of school education. Further discussion of these steps which can be undertaken by practicing teachers are given here-in-after.

10.1 Stating *Success Indicators* in Observable Terms

(a) *Knowledge of Success Indicators:* In order to know the success or failure of a system of school based assessment the most significant evidence is to show whether the observed outcomes are in accordance with the indicators of success. In other words we are to be very clear about what are intended success indicators of good quality education against which we can judge, the observed outcomes of a good system of S.B.A. Such indicators may be in terms of cognitive and non-cognitive outcomes. The congruence or discrepancy between the intended and the observed learning outcomes would show the quality of SBA system used or the observed impact on students' learning.

(i) Statement of success indicators in advance is necessary to provide the direction for the practicing teachers and the basis of assessing students to find out as to how far the system of SBA has lead to the achievement of those criteria or intended outcomes. In the absence of such statement of success indicators it will not be possible for teachers to direct their teaching learning activities towards intended indicators of success which indeed become the focal points for providing basis of assessment. In the absence of such indicators it will not be possible to select relevant teaching learning strategies which lead to the development of intended learning outcomes. Therefore, cognizance of success indicators becomes the basis, focus and direction for teaching learning activities to provide relevant learning experiences.

(ii) Of course these indicators should be stated in observable terms both for cognitive and non-cognitive aspects of pupils' development. In case of non-cognitive or co-scholastic aspects quality control measures are to be reflected in terms of habits to be cultivated, interests to be inculcated, attitudes to be developed and other personal social qualities considered desirable for holistic development of learners. In case of cognitive or scholastic aspects of measurement, the outcomes intended are to be stated in a way that reflect the competencies which are expected to be developed as a result of efficient and effective teaching and learning. Such a list of competencies stated represent the intended outcomes that become the basis of assessment, called the competency based assessment preceded by the competency based teaching.

(b) *Criteria for Curriculum Weightage*: Depending on the nature and scope of the subject in a given curriculum, weightages in terms of credit points, marks allotted, time allotted and other criteria have also to be reflected keeping in view the importance of various aspects of learners' development reflected in the prescribed curriculum objectives. This would vary from subject to subject.

(i) Success indicators are to be stated at the subject level by the curriculum and evaluation experts and at unit level by the teachers cooperatively while at the lesson level the concerned teacher has to state these indicators himself in terms of intended learning outcomes which are observable or measurable.

(ii) How to know that these success indicators are relevant and attainable for a particular group of students studying at a particular stage? This can be judged through students' performance when analyzed in terms of stated indicators or criteria of success at lesson, unit area and total syllabus level. At lesson level oral readiness' testing, class questioning, students' questions, sectional recapitulation, school assignments and home assignment can be used to test students' performance that reflect quality of their responses. At unit level, students' performance on unit test based on unit-wise stated competencies, can be analyzed. Similarly students' performance on area-wise and total syllabus can be analyzed to judge in terms of stated competencies to know whether instructional impact has been as intended in terms of observed outcomes. At the same time pupils' performance in terms of stated indicators would also reflect whether their performance on different indicators is in general poor, satisfactory, good or outstanding.

(c) *Judging Relevance of Stated Success Indicators*

(i) One major problem that may arise is that of interpretation and judgmenting on the relevance of the stated success indicators. High or exceptionally high performance of students may be due to low difficulty level of the question paper set by the teacher. Likewise, poor or very poor performance of students on different indicators may again be due to high difficulty level of the question paper set.

(ii) Unless balanced question paper are set, inferences drawn may be questionable. In fact competency-wise (success indicators) analysis of students' performance over the whole year when summative evaluation is done as in semester or annual promotion examination, if undertaken cooperatively by a group of schools would provide more substantive and reliable evidence about pupils' performance on each success indicator.

(iii) Nevertheless, success indicators stated to improve quality of SBA have to be validated and revalidated from time to time because of changing emphasis in instructional objectives, assessment tools and techniques, prescribed syllabi and instructional objectives at a particular level. Therefore, review of success indicators and validating them from time to time in accordance with the changing emphases is necessary to make institution based assessment more valid, dependable and practicable.

(d) Use of relevant mode of evaluation at appropriate stages of teaching learning process also contribute to the quality of education. At the planning stage rational evaluation involving evaluation and curriculum experts and educational administrators is necessary to get consensus on all issues related to SBA. Formative evaluation by practicing teachers to get regular feedback about students' learning and summative evaluation undertaken cooperatively involving evaluation experts is essential to gather evidences about students' achievement, making judgments and taking decisions for improving further students' learning and instructional strategies.

(e) For improving quality of education through school based system of assessment it is necessary that teaching learning strategies to be adopted should be such that teachers remain cognizant of what for they are going to test i.e. the purpose of testing; when should they test to gather intended evidences about pupils' learning; what are the most relevant measures and tools of assessment to be used and how to ensure intra and inter-school cooperation for assessment. This could definitely improve the validity and reliability of the evidences collected.

(f) Proper motivation of students, their encouragement and involvement in assessment, emphasis on their self-assessment, self-referenced judgment, provision of flexibility in undertaking examination, avoiding labelling them as failures or under achievers, giving more opportunities for self-learning and helping them for learning how to learn are all significant action tasks, for improving students' quality of learning.

(g) Another quality improvement measure is to develop and use quality resource material like school based question banks, which can be developed cooperatively by different schools. Use of ready made question banks developed by D.I.E.T.S, S.C.E.R.T.s or other educational agencies can also be made use of in case of term and annual tests. Resource material in the form of quizzes, school and home assignments, testing higher order abilities, exemplars of competency based questions on different competencies implied by knowledge, understanding (comprehension in language) and application (written expression in language) objective etc. would go a long way to help teachers to improve quality of education.

(h) The most significant step is to get regular feedback of instructional impact of the various programmes undertaken and know the inadequacies for further improvement. For this undertaking *programme evaluation* is very relevant. Each programme undertaken must be judged by teachers, students' reactions and experts' views at the planning stage through summative evaluation. Programme evaluation helps to validate pupils' achievement and provides ideas, problems, issues relating to efficiency and effectiveness of teaching learning process.

(i) To some extent it is also the financial resources that impact the quality programes. Therefore, we have to ensure that all programmes undertaken to improve quality of education are cost effective.

10.2 Adopting Sustainable Strategy of Implementation

Using S.B.A. for promoting of education pre-supposes that the system of assessment has to be focussed on the cognition of intended educational outcomes stated in the form of success indicators which indeed provide the needed direction. However, equally important is the implementation strategy. If it is not sustainable, results expected may not accrue to the desired extent. Therefore, for implementation of S.B.A. system following measures are relevant for improving quality of education.

(a) Study of the stated success indicators in details to see whether all of them are relevant and applicable to all the subjects in the school. The more the subject teachers are involved in discussion, adaptation and final acceptance the better it is for implementing it.

(b) For effective implementation and sustainability reform in establishing good system of S.B.A. it is desirable that phasing of reference be undertaken stage wise, i.e. elementary stage to start with and followed by secondary stage. The better it is to start at primary, then middle and leading to secondary stage, because at primary stage 100 per cent is internal assessment, mostly as integral part of teaching and learning. Similarly phasing may be undertaken with respect to assessment of scholastic aspects of pupils' development followed by co-scholastic aspects, after having gained some experience of valid assessment of curricular area or units of study. Moreover, for assessment of co-scholastic aspects further training or orientation of teachers may be called for.

(c) Since different stakeholders of reform are concerned with the impact of improved internal assessment their involvement in various decision making process is valuable to improve the system of assessment in terms of its implementation and public acceptability. Learners, peers, parents, principals, community, supervisors and administrators all of them have stakes in success of the scheme.

(d) Proper standard setting in terms of intended learning outcomes is another criterion of quality education as reflected in the form of desired success indicators. The more the higher order competencies are considered desirable for learners, the better the standards are set in a subject prescribed for learners, the prescribed substantive structure of the discipline concerned remaining the same. Of course it is through summative evaluation of students' performance from time to time that we can judge whether standard set are achieved and are achievable.

(e) Attainment targeting is also necessary in terms of frequency, time frame and nature of assessment to be undertaken, tools of assessments, mode of grading or marking and getting timely feed back on all assessments and readjustment of targets are to undertaken. In fact a calendar of assessment related action tasks is to be developed cooperatively for guidance of teachers.

10.3 Using Reflective, Formative and Summative Evaluation

Since evaluation is an integral part of teaching learning process its purpose is not only to measure students' achievements but also to use it for improving their achievement. Of course its use, as a judgmental device to certify their achievement for promotion or selection purposes, cannot be undermined. Therefore, depending upon the various stages of instruction or curriculum transactions different modes of evaluation are used to improve quality of teaching learning process vis-à-vis learning and instruction.

(a) *Rational or Reflective Evaluation*

It is at the planning stage of every programme, project and other instructional inputs that decisions are taken by teachers involving co-teachers, students, parents, community members and subject experts. It is democratic and illuminative mode of evaluation based on experience and consensus of the stakeholders. This mode of logical evaluation is undertaken during planning. When to evaluate; for what to evaluate and how best to evaluate pupils are to be decided only on the basis of expert opinion, views of teachers and logical analysis of intended learning outcomes which form the basis of teaching and learning. Focus is on taking cognizance of quality indicators.

(b) *Formative Evaluation*

It is the integral part of teaching learning strategies, used at various stages of instruction focus of which is on getting and providing feedback about learners' achievement and instructional impact. Use of readiness tests for better placement, using higher order questions during teaching as an instructional device or for recapitulation of what is taught, and students' questioning during instructional phase are all meant to improve quality of learning and instruction. Use of higher order competency based questions in the classroom by teachers leads students to ask higher order ability questions. Likewise good assignments involving higher order ability questions lead to better enforcement of students' learning besides getting feedback about quality of responses related to assignment. Main focus of formative evaluation is on the improvement of students' achievements.

(c) *Summative Evaluation*

Focus of summative evaluation remains on judging students in terms of intended learning outcomes. Whether it is a unit test, term test or an annual test the decisions are taken on the basis of judgments formed abut students' performance. Purpose is to take decision for promotion, certification, selection, for admission to courses of studies etc. All annual tests conducted by school, public examination conducted by boards, universities and selection agencies come under summative evaluation which provide evidences about congruence or discrepancy between intended and observed outcomes that reflect the quality of instruction as well as of students' learning, both cognitive and non-cognitive.

To improve quality of summative evaluation use of question banks in developing quality written tests can be taken advantage of. In order to improve quality of intended outcomes we have to assure that efforts, efficiency and effectiveness are up to the mark during curriculum transactions, programmes undertaken or other processes adopted. Therefore, during different phases of planning, development, implementation and quality control it becomes necessary for quality assurance, that rational evaluation during planning, formative evaluation during implementation and summative evaluation during judgmental phase are to be undertaken to reflect on pupils' performance and restricted to paper pencil tests. It is, therefore necessary that for improving the quality of process and quality of products we have to understand the role of logical, formative and summative evaluation at various stages for different purposes. Nevertheless, we have to ensure quality of assessment devices. In view of predominance of the use of written examinations and on going project of developing and using question banks in testing, especially for summative purpose is the need of our teacher evaluators.

10.4 Undertaking Diagnostic Testing and Remedial Instruction

As mentioned earlier formative evaluation in the form of class questioning, class assignments, unit testing and even term tests provide regular feed back to teachers about pupils' adequacies and inadequacies in learning or achievement. Criteria of a good evaluation is the diagnostic use of the results otherwise evaluation cannot be dynamic. Therefore, to improve quality of students' learning we have to analyze results to identify under achievers as well as areas of weakness. Lack, of readiness to learn causes difficulty for such students to benefit fully from instruction. What are the learning difficulties or deficiencies and what are the causes of such deficiencies? Achievement tests help to identify under achievers whereas diagnostic tests pin point specific areas of weakness or difficulty. Of course in certain cases intelligence level of a student can be the limited factor. Likewise, other non-cognitive or non-academic reasons for low performance may be due to lack of proper work habits, lack of interest, and positive attitudes, physical health, or maladjustment of the learners. Even average or above average students who score below their capacity have to be diagnosed and guided properly. Teacher observations, testing and interviews with students help to diagnose nature of difficulties. We have to look for such students whose achievement gap between expected and actual achievement is there so that remedial measures may be undertaken.

(a) *Development of Diagnostic Tests*

Improvement in performance of underachievers is best possible when diagnostic tests are developed in such areas identified through achievement testing. Such tests cover all learning points in sequential order. These tests are more structured than achievement tests and provide detailed picture of strategies and weakness of students in specified areas. Development of diagnostic tests involve four main steps.

(i) Analysis of content and process into components or learning points in order of complexity;
(ii) Development of test items on the components of learning points by writing 3 or 5 items on each learning point;
(iii) Assembling the test in order of the complexity of learning points; and
(iv) Administering the test and analysing students' performance.

(b) *Undertaking* Remedial Measures

Once the analysis of diagnostic test is done remedial measures are taken which may be individual or group based. Depending upon the under achievers the basis adopted for remediation is to improve achievement of the learner by his proper placement in learning sequence, hastening the process, reinforcing and feedback of learning outcomes. This requires:

(i) identifying the pre-requisite behaviours,
(ii) using readiness test or analysis of performance on previous unit tests,
(iii) identifying poor performers, causes of poor performance to classify them in terms of their needs,
(iv) using diagnostic tests, analysis and interpreting data,
(v) providing for alternative strategies for remediation,
(vi) regular and immediate feed back after testing, and
(vii) providing suitable correchieves to bring the under achievers to the optimum level.

Improvement in performance of students, particularly under achievers would be possible and remediation would be better if the diagnostic tests are properly constructed and learning points arranged in order of complexity. Since it is difficult for all the practicing teachers to construct such diagnostic tests it is for the department to organize training courses for them to develop such tests, analyse and use relevant remedial instructions. This diagnostic evaluation at various stages for various areas to identify underachievers and the areas of weakness is essential to improve quality of instruction vis-à-vis students' achievement. Need for exemplar material cannot be undermined.

10.5 Applying Quality Control Measures for Better Assessment

Purpose of applying quality control measures is that a teacher should be able to gather needed information about learners' learning faithfully, form proper judgments about pupils' performance and then take timely proper decisions about learners, instruction and assessment process. This involves a number of action tasks which have to be taken cognizance of by the practicing teachers. Measures like the following have to be taken to improve quality of assessment.

(a) Making evaluation an integral part of teaching learning process. It is possible by using questioning as a teaching device. However, use of higher order ability questions by teachers is significant for improving students' learning and encouraging them to develop better learning.

(b) Cognizance of purpose of assessment is a pre-requisite for taking up any assessment programme. Is it diagnostic, getting feedback about students' learning? Is it for grading students? Is it for selection purpose ? Is it for certification of students' achievement ? This would provide direction for stating success indicators in the form of intended learning outcomes reflecting the competencies the students will be expected to develop.

(c) In case of rational evaluation attempt should be made to involve subject related experts as well as some stakeholders of reform. In case of formative evaluation, students and co-teachers must be consulted so that intended inputs are used for getting and providing needed feedback. In case of summative evaluation quality of assessment can be improved through cooperative designing of the test, and use of high quality questions from good question banks, to collect valid and reliable evidences.

(d) For analysis of performance of students, it is necessary to analyse evidence in terms of intended learning outcomes and still better is that pupils' performance is judged in terms of competencies implied in different objectives. This would help us to know quality of performance in terms of students' achievement in higher order competencies, as compared to performance on lower level competencies.

(e) How best to process the evidence for meaningful reporting is also essential to reflect quality of performance. Therefore, depending upon the purpose self-referenced, criterion referenced, or norm-referenced judgments have to be made.

(f) Use of remedial measures in accordance with the evidences, gathered through observations, diagnostic testing etc. is the main quality measure of improving students' achievements. As per analysis of evidences individual or group-wise remedial instruction may be provided.

(g) The basic quality measure is to use the assessment measures, which are valid and reliable to ensure evidence about pupils, that is dependable. Unless quality of measuring instruments or tools and techniques used for data gathering, is good no proper inference about pupils' performance can be drawn.

(h) In case of data collection through observations it is all the more necessary that subjectivity of observers does not reign supreme. Use of proper observation schedule by more than one observer becomes necessary to ensure dependable evidence.

(i) Cooperative and participative testing can further improve quality of assessment. This can be undertaken by developing quality question banks in various subjects and involving intra-school and inter-school teachers in developing assessment devices and having inter-school cooperative testing once or twice a year. Besides ensuring better quality of assessment it provides genuine comparability of inter school students' performance.

(j) The most critical analysis of students' performance reveals discrepancies between the intended and the observed objectives. Likewise, it reflects on the structure of the subjects which may require some changes in the syllabus. Indirectly it reflects on the impact of teaching learning strategies adopted. Thus in a way the whole teaching learning process is validated according to which improvements in instructional objectives, content of subject and teaching learning strategies can be made, while reviewing the assessment system.

10.6 Using Evaluation as Feedback Device for Improving Teaching Learning Process

Evaluation is a process of collecting evidences, forming judgments and taking decisions. All decision are taken on the basis of feed back reflected in terms of students' performance on the intended outcomes which form the basis of assessment. In the context of the teaching learning process various types of feed back could be got by teachers, depending upon the purpose of assessment, area of assessment, instructional strategies used in teaching learning process and the mode and techniques employed for assessing students. In each case a particular type of feedback is possible which forms the basis of improvement.

(a) Analysis of over all evidences gathered about students' performance through various assessment devices, provides feedback in terms of stated intended learning outcomes usually prescribed in terms of instructional objectives in each subject, in the prescribed curriculum. Feedback on students' performance on different objectives provide the basis for needed improvement on some assessment objectives. May be continuous low performance of students particularly good performers, on certain stated objectives or competencies listed under these objectives, reflect the need for review of such objectives or competencies which might have been pitched high.

(b) Analysis may also reveal about the relevance of the substantive structure of a subject. Students' performance on various content elements also provide good feed back about relevance of concepts, principles, processes, themes etc. Moreover, diagnostic evaluation provide feed back on selected content elements which can be made the basis for improving students' performance on such concepts in which further improvement through remediation could be undertaken.

(c) In case curriculum transactions evaluation provides feed back on various assessment modes adopted in teaching and learning process, and other programmes undertaken to supplement teaching learning process. In case of instruction, evaluation of students for readiness of instruction using readiness test, (oral or written), questioning as a teaching device or for getting feedback about learners and use relevant measures like re-teaching, remedial teaching, providing exemplar material etc. Another significance feedback through evaluation is about programmes organized by the teachers to corborate teaching eg. excursion, debate, quizzes, development of question pool, inter-or intra school cooperative testing etc. For each programme evaluation in terms of inputs provides evidences about students' inputs and participation, which helps to improve further the teaching learning process.

(d) Feedback of assessment of students through testing in the form of unit tests, diagnostic tests, term tests or annual tests conducted by teachers provide useful evidence for improving teaching learning process. Feedback through unit testing provides adequacies or inadequacies of students in a given area which provides basis for diagnostic testing when causes of recurring inadequacies are to be discovered so that accordingly remedial teaching could be adopted. In case of summative testing like term and annual test analysis of students' performance does reveal certain content areas as well as instructional objectives in which students are underachievers or have very poor performance. This also provides basis for undertaking relevant measures, or even require some review of the syllabus and instructional objectives to update it.

(e) School learning environments also impact students' performance. Therefore, evaluation of total school learning environment by cooperative efforts of administrative and academic staff involving students and other stake holders has to be undertaken. It would help to get feed back on setting, inputs, processes, out puts and impact of school learning environments and would reflect the need for review to improve the existing environments for better learning.

To Sum up

From the above discussion it is quite evident that evaluation is a process which can be used as a feed back device for improving teaching learning process. Such a feed back may be used to make instructional objectives more practicable and validate curriculum content to make syllabus more relevant. Likewise, feed back about efficiency of curriculum transactions, programmes undertaken and even evaluation techniques and tools, and school learning environment, can be taken advantage of, to improve the existing system and make it more efficient and effective.

11

Undertaking Institutional Self-Evaluation (I.S.E.)

11.1 Nature, Purpose and Scope of I.S.E.

(a) *School Self-Evaluation* is a planned, cooperatively organized, inquiry carried out by school teachers, students and principals of the institution to judge the effectiveness of the various operations and activities of the institution. Purpose is to find out the adequacies and inadequacies of the various processes and products of performance on the basis of which needed steps could be taken to improve the existing practices of teaching, learning and assessment. It is in a way an attempt to make judgment on the learning environments of the school and take decisions to improve teaching, learning and assessment practices.

(b) I.S.E. cannot be equated with continuous comprehensive evaluation although it is also school based assessment. Focus of C.C.E. is on pupils' assessment which includes, concept, model, assessment procedures, measuring tools and techniques, marking, grading and reporting of subject-wise results of pupils. Whereas focus of C.C.E. is on pupils' assessment and their improvement in learning or achievement, focus of I.S.E. is on judging the school's effectiveness in terms of evaluating the institution as a whole not alone the students' performance. Its scope is therefore, not limited to assessment of students but extends to total school learning environments.

(c) Aim is to determine holistic view of the efforts made, efficiency with which efforts are made and the effectiveness of the institution as a whole. Besides gathering information about pupils' attainments instructional impact made by teachers in terms of teaching learning strategies used by them are also included. Other assessment factors to judge are as to how effective was the learning environments of the school, how best financial, academic and administrative resources were utilized, and how far such factors and conditions that contribute to or hinder different school processes, were taken care of during the session or the academic year. Ultimate focus remains on judging total school effectiveness so that appropriate measures are taken to improve the existing conditions vis-à-vis social learning milieu of the school to promote better teaching learning processes.

(d) For effective I.S.E. comprehensive, cooperative and systemic evaluation efforts have to be made by the staff of the institution. It requires identification of the problems and issues that impact students' achievement. Accordingly, desirable and positive changes are to be introduced to improve students' learning and instructional strategies.

(e) Basis of such improvement through institutional self-evaluation is in agreement with the formative summative model of Scriven (1972). The frame work of this model aims at:

   (i) understanding of the strengths and weaknesses of the institution in terms of intended or stated learning outcomes or success indicators as well as social responsibility of the institution.

   (ii) vitalizing the various educational processes to improve students' performance as well as its outputs.

   (iii) reflecting focus of I.S.E. is on updating the stated intended aims and validate in terms of performance indicators so that discrepancy if any between the intended and the observed outcomes is minimized.

Idea of I.S.E. is to improve quality of out puts as also pupils' performance. Such as institutional self-study can be undertaken annually or on alternate year to get at the issues, problems, possibilities, solutions and review the ongoing policies, framework of curriculum transaction, assessment objectives and feedback processes for improving students' achievement and instructional effectiveness. It is, therefore necessary that the school authorities in general and practicing teachers in particular school be well acquainted with the essential characteristic of institutional self-evaluation, discussed here-in-after.

11.2 Assessment Components in Institutional Self-Evaluation

Besides the social milieu of an institution there are other factors which condition learning as well as instruction and assessments. A number of programmes are organized in the school but it is seldom that these programmes are evaluated to judge their impact or effectiveness. It is taken for granted that, the seminars, workshops or learning courses organized for teachers, paper setters, examiners, writers of textbook chapters etc. are good and successful. Sometimes a few open-ended questions are given to participants to get their opinion about the quality of the programme which indeed provides very scanty idea of programme effectiveness. What actually is required is to assess each programme, activity, or project, in terms of its context or setting, the inputs given, processes undertaken, out puts or product accrued and the impact it made on the participants. It is therefore, necessary that before taking any decision about the effectiveness of a programme we have to address the following components for assessment purpose.

(a) *Evaluating the context*: This refers to the following:

(i) School setting, its locale, centrally located, or faraway, approach etc.
(ii) Social context in terms of community participation, linkage with local education authorities, N.G.Os. etc.
(iii) Historical perspective in terms of results of students, reputation for co-curricular activities for developing co-scholastic aspects.
(iv) Antecedents of the programmes undertaken and previous experiences.

(b) *Evaluating the inputs*: This refers to inputs like the following:

(i) Expertise and qualifications of the personnel involved in programmes
(ii) Instructional and other materials provided to the practitioners
(iii) Research and other support services provided
(iv) Time spent on various tasks and activities
(v) Financial and human resources provided

(c) *Evaluating the processes undertaken*: This refers to processes like the following:

(i) Cognizance of the assessment objectives
(ii) Competency based testing and teaching
(iii) Efforts made by teachers in terms of using teaching, learning and testing material.
(iv) Efficiency with which the tasks were undertaken.
(v) Effectiveness of processes undertaken by involving other persons and the expertise availed of.

(d) *Evaluating the outcomes or products*: This refers to outputs like the following:

(i) Attainment of programme objectives in terms of students' performance
(ii) Quality of material produced, reports published etc.
(iii) Growth and development of staff; participants and other clientele

(iv) Cost effectiveness of the programmes
(v) Interests and attitudes developed towards the programmes

(e) *Evaluating the impact of programmes*: It refers to programmes like the following:

(i) Improved teaching learning practices
(ii) Improved assessment practices
(iii) Better learning environment of the school
(iv) Better community support in school processes
(v) Better parents' concern and students' involvement in teaching learning practices

Idea of I.S.E. is to find out how far the various programmes undertaken have proved to be effective to achieve the set objectives and attain the set targets in terms of students' learning and instructional strategies adopted. And for that what sort of assessment objectives are applicable. Never-the-less, it is the social responsibility of the institution and its care takers to provide the needed guidance, support and resources. It is in this context that in evaluating an institution by the staff, students and other stakeholders, concerned with improvement of the institution have to assess and find out problems, issues and other concerns related to education of the students. For this we have to find out as to what extent schools setting; is favourable, inputs given are adequate, teaching learning processes are efficient, outcome or product accrued are congruent with intended or stated objectives and the impact-made on the interest and altitudes of all stakeholders is relevant or acceptable in view of human resources and financial in puts, Next step is to think of the approach to be used for data collection while evaluating the institution.

11.3 Pluralistic Approaches for Data Collection and Processing

For institutional self-evaluation following characteristics are essential:

(a) ***Using Pluralistic Approach***

(i) This is necessary for collection of data, processing and analysis of data and for review of programmes or action tasks.

(ii) Identify institutional clientele who are interested and ready to take part in the study and help in data collection and analysis of problems that require proper attention.

(iii) Selected stake holders like students, parents, community members, supervisors, counsellors, administrators and others can be identified who will be involved in institutional self-evaluation.

(iv) These participants will help the institutional staff to identify specific problems faced by the institution and help in finding out or suggesting solutions to those problems.

(b) ***Using Psychometric and Descriptive Approaches***

For collection of data and processing the same we can take advantage of approaches like the following:

(i) Collection of extensive data relevant to various issues using various modes and assessment devices followed by analysis of data and interpreting the same to reflect the needed improvement related to problems identified.

(ii) Open discussion on concerned issues and problems can be organized among the participant observers. This would highlight the view points of the participants for improving the learning environments of the institution.

(iii) Sometimes it is useful to generate emotional interaction of teachers, parents, community, principals and supervisors in order to gather free and frank opinion or views of these participant observers.

(iv) Using of course evaluation tools and techniques to gather needed information, for judgmenting and taking decisions regarding improvements to be made in assessment process.

(v) Providing research support in respect of various issues and existing practices as well as suggested changes would definitely reflect on existing practices and on suggested ones.

(c) *Using Reports and Other Documentary Evidences*

This is another mode of institutional self-evaluation which refers to tasks like the following:

(i) Analysis of reports of inspectors or supervisors' visiting the institution during the year which does provide some significant evidence in the form of their views reflected concerning inadequacies or strengths of the school practices.

(ii) Another way to assess performance of an institution is to compare inter-institutional cooperative testing results which reflects efforts and efficiency of the educational processes adopted by an institution. Similarly inter-school comparison of students' results in the board's examination is another mode of institutional self-evaluation.

(iii) Reports of management committees and governing bodies are also relevant to reflect on effectiveness of the school apparatus in terms of intended and stated objectives. It is these committees or bodies which provide the leadership and guidance to the school personnel to ensure achievement of intended outcomes.

From the above discussions, regarding use of pluralistic approach, psychometric and descriptive approaches and various types of reports and documentary evidences as evidenced in inter school comparative testing and board results, are all relevant means to gather evidences reflecting the effectiveness of school learning environment that become integral part of institutional self-evaluation.

11.4 Undertaking *Humanistic Illuminative Evaluation*

(a) Humanistic Illuminative Evaluation based on social anthropological paradigm is concerned with description and interpretation rather than measurement and prediction. It attempts to document, as a participant observer; how does a programme work and is influenced by the varying situations in the school.

(b) For understanding illuminative evaluation the two central concepts are the *instructional system* and the *learning milieu* of the school. Those personnel who are involved in this process and the various constraints and conditions under which a project works in the class room are the basis of evaluation.

(c) Such a humanistic illuminative evaluation involves views, opinions and concerns of all stake holders of school community. In fact besides the institutional community many other persons who are engaged in different ways to improve educational process of the school are equally concerned whose views are of great importance. All stakeholders and participant observers whose involvement is of significance include:

(i) *Principals, staff members, students and auxiliary staff:* These members of school community are of greatest importance since their opinion is based on their maximum involvement in the various educational processes focused on attainment of the instructional objectives and assessment of students as they interact with each other daily.

(ii) *Managing committees, representatives of parent teachers associations and community representatives:* The members representing these committees, associations and other representative from organizations like S.C.E.R.T. and examining boards, who are involved off and on, do provide technical, academic and management guidelines for improving efficiency and effectiveness of school practices vis-à-vis learning milieu.

(iii) *Employers, school illumini and representatives of colleges*: Besides participant observers, there are other people or observers who can provide their considered experience based views on improving the existing system of assessment and instructional strategies. Different types of employers can provide the opinion and guidance about the intended requirements of different vocations. School alumni can share their experience and needed improvement for better achievement and assessment.

Like-wise representatives from colleges and other institutions, where students are supposed to get admission after schooling, can surely provide realistic intended requirements in terms of expected capabilities which should be developed in schools. Thus it can be taken cognizance of in institutional self-evaluations.

(iv) *Curriculum and evaluation experts and subject specialists*: Opinion of various subject experts who are supposed to be well familiar with the substantive structure of the subject would be able to provide specific guidelines for better teaching of concepts and principles in their respective field of study. Like-wise, curriculum experts will be able to provide how best curriculum objectives are formulated, curriculum content or syllabus is developed and taught; and how best curriculum transactions are carried out for better teaching.

Evaluation experts would help how best data are collected, processed and interpreted, how best self-referenced, criterion-referenced and norm-referenced judgments are made and right decisions taken for grading and certification of students. Therefore, involvement of these professional experts during institutional self-evaluation would go a long way to identify the areas of strengths and weaknesses in terms of school setting, school inputs, school processes, school outputs and impact evaluation. Of course their role is not judgementing but limited to counseling and guidance.

Illuminative evaluation which represents sociological approach is based on complex interaction of various parameters having bearing on pupils' learning while judgments are formed as per consensus of all those who are participant observers in the teaching learning process. In a way institutional self-study is an in house evaluation which is formative in nature and poses no threat to the staff of the institution. Its suggestions are more likely to be accepted and implemented and would go a longway to ensure attainment of intended instructional objectives. Therefore, need for seminars and workshops to execute efficiently the institutional self-studies on regular basis cannot be over-emphasized to make institutions more aware of their usefulness.

11.5 Using Institutional Self-evaluation for Improving Schools' Learning Environment

Institutional self-study, if scientifically conducted in the context of social milieu of the school, provides a number of indicators of success and failures. Inadequacies in terms of students' results as compared to the previous years and other schools located in the same block of district are reflected. Similarly students' performance on co-scholastic aspects, in terms of activities and programmes organized, can also indicate the adequacies or inadequacies; as reflected in their study and work habits, interest developed in studies, attitude towards studies, teachers and other students besides other personality traits.

Students' performance in various subject areas in terms of their performance on different units also provides evidence about the content areas where more teacher inputs are required and diagnostic evaluation is called for to find out the causes of poor performance.

This study would also reflect instructional impact of effectiveness of the teaching learning strategies adopted. Of course we assume that assessment made do have reasonable validity and reliability and evidences gathered are dependable. On the basis of such evidences revealed through institutional self-study we can further improve learning environments of the school by adopting measures like the following:

(a) *Improving the Physical Facilities*

Analysis of I.S.E. study would reveal whether in view of students' intake the physical facilities in the schools are adequate for their physical development and proper study. Do we need more space for classrooms? Do we need better equipment and furniture for better and comfortable sitting? Do we have proper playground for students and provision for organizing various games? Do we have properly and adequately equipped laboratories, libraries etc.? If not, provision for such and other related facilities will have to be provided for improving the existing environments.

(b) *Availability of Academic resources:*

(i) I.S.E. study would also provide evidence about the adequacy, quality and inputs given during the academic year. Do we have needed students' intake in our school or we have mostly students from poor families or more students are admitted than the physical facilities available. Apart from that more significant step in terms of learning environment is whether students respect each other, learn from each other and cooperate with each other. Are students involved in some decision taking processes like organization of examinations, programmes and activities etc.? What are the adopted means to motivate the students' for better learning? Are students dubbed as underachievers, poor performers, third divisioners, failures etc which makes them feel socially out caste. Focus indeed should not be on highlighting their weaknesses but their strong points (eg. good sports boy, very disciplined, regular in classes, respects teachers etc) so as to make them feel good and improve their achievement.

- To what extent teachers have succeeded in achieving the instructional objectives will also be known when results of students are analysed in terms of developed and underdeveloped competencies. How far assessment mode, rational and formative used to collect needed evidences, are used to improve students' performance? To what extent he involved students in teaching learning process and encouraged students to highlight the good points of poor performers, and did not use terms like failure or underachievers. Has he ever used diagnostic tests? What additional reading from educational journals he has done to improve his proficiency in teaching. Answer to such questions reflect on improving learning environment. I.S.E. should also reveal whether the principal of the school has been able to provide all possible academic resources and guidance to teachers. A good library, a journal on education, organizing seminar or workshop for empowerment of teachers and establishing linkages with educational agencies like N.C.E.R.T., S.C.E.R.T., D.I.E.T. examining agencies etc. are relevant functions which are to taken care of to improve learning environments of the institution.

- How best the supervisors, inspectors and other educational administrators have provided the needed guidelines and provided the teachers technical support for improved teaching and testing? Have they been able to organize inter-school testing programme for better comparison of studies' performance and establish parity of performance standard? If not role of supervisors has to be reviewed and accordingly reoriented.
- How best the assessment system in the school was carried out, as revealed in I.S.E. study needs to be analysed. Did the school undertake humanistic illuminative evaluation besides the psychometric traditional approach for formative and summative evaluation? Was cooperative testing undertaken for better comparison of interschool students'

performance? Was any attempt made to develop school based question bank involving students and utilized the same in summative testing in term or annual examination?

- Another analysis of I.S.E. study would also reveal the efforts and efficiency with which various management tasks were undertaken by the management committee of the school. Was adequate financial support provided for various programmes and projects? Was proper coordination among various personnel in different areas of action tasks, carried on? Did monitoring and evaluation lead to the intended learning outcome or other outputs? Did the managing committee encourage teaching staff and help them to improve their qualification and professional efficiency? Did the management provide or encourage the staff to use research and other support services to improve students' learning and validate intended learning outcomes.

To Conclude

Thus we find that undertaking institutional self-evaluation provides all type of relevant evidences of various issues and educational processes carried on in the school during the previous year. Analysis of evidences gathered in I.S.E. reflect impact on students' learning and other action tasks carried out by the principals, teaching staff, students and supervisors on the basis of the inadequacies of the stakeholders of school and the needed improvement in various areas. It is possible to improve further the learning environments of the institution using cooperative participative strategy for achieving the intended learning outcomes.

12

Providing Research and Other Support Services

12.1 Nature, Purpose and Scope of Research in S.B.A.

(a) Best defines 'research as the systematic and objective analysis and recording of controlled observations that may lead to the development of generalisations and principles or theories resulting in prediction and possibly ultimate control of events'. Some significant characteristics of research are:

- Research is directed towards the solution of a problem. Goal being to discover cause and effect relationship between variable it emphasises development of principles, generalization and theories.
- It is based on empirical evidence and demands accurate observation which may be quantitative or qualitative. It involves collection of new data from primary sources or using existing data for a new purpose and is characterized by carefully designed procedure requiring rigorous analysis. It is carefully recorded and reported.

(b) *Purpose of Research*: Goal of *basic* research is to develop theories and apply the findings to actual problems in those areas which are considered to be the concern of the people. Purpose of *applied* research is to improve a process or a product and test theoretical concepts in actual problem situation. Mostly educational research is applied research as it attempts to develop generalizations about teaching learning processes. *Action* research is not focussed on development of theory but its emphasis is on immediate application of problems here and now. Teachers if involved in research activity are in the area of action research.

(c) Three types of educational research studies can be categorized under one or a combination of the following three types:

- *Historical research* which describes what was. Process involves investigation, analysis and interpretation of past events for discovering the generalization to understand that past and present and to a limited extent anticipating the future.
- *Descriptive research* describes what is and describes, records analysis and interprets the conditions that exist. It involves comparison or contrast and discovers relationships between existing variables which are non-manipulative.
- *Experimental research* which describes what will be, when certain variables are carefully controlled or manipulated. Focus is on variable relationships and deliberate manipulation.

After having understood the nature, purpose and scope of research in terms of various types of researches applicable in the field of education let us see how we can use different types of researches in improving the existing system of school based assessment. In fact at the school level basic or fundamental research has no scope since it cannot be undertaken by teachers'.

Nevertheless, there are certain areas of investigations which can be undertaken by some teachers who want to do Ph.D. in education in the field of assessment. For example in the field of assessment objectives, we usually follow N.C.E.R.T. taxonomy in India. Topics like the following can be undertaken for basic research.

- An investigation into the cumulative hierarchy of N.C.E.R.T. taxonomy of educational objectives in science subjects at the secondary stage.

Such a study would help to validate this taxonomy and help in making this taxonomy more usable in updating assessment objectives.

- In certain cases even applied research projects can also be undertaken by some teachers to improve existing processes or products and test certain theoretical concepts related to actual problems. For example:
  To investigate the hierarchy of competencies listed under the three objectives of knowledge, understanding and application for stated in N.C.E.R.T. taxonomy.
- In case of action research project like the following may be undertaken.
  To investigate the reliability of the test in terms of students' performance on various competencies included under different assessment objectives (knowledge, understanding and application) in biology.

Primary class room teachers can more easily identify the assessment problems with which they are confronted. Such problems can become the basis of investigation under action research. For example in an open ended question given as home assignment or set in a formative test like unit test, one may encounter problem of scoring. Should he allot 5, 10, 15 or 20 marks for each question? Which one would be more reliable? Here a problem like the following emerges for investigation, the solution of which is required here and now i.e. applicable to scoring reliability.

- To investigate the scheme of marking an open ended/ essay type question in terms of allotment of marks to such questions, (10, 15, 20). For example once we find that allotting 20 marks to each question leads to more reliable marking, the teacher get evidence through action research. This is how various assessment related problems emerge during classroom testing, unit testing and term tests etc. which can be solved by teachers themselves through action research. They can take help of some evaluation experts or other educationists from different agencies to develop the research proposal and then carry on.

It would indeed be very good if research is used to identify the problems as well as for finding solution to those problems. Of course teachers have to remain cognizant of the problem that arises during assessment and then finding out the solution by discovering the causes through action research.

12.2 Inter-Institutional Cooperative Research Project

It has already been emphasized earlier that it is necessary to use research support to improve school based assessment. Beside individual institution based research studies we can even undertake inter-institutional cooperative research projects, involving one, two or more institutions and even in certain studies all the schools in a block depending upon the scope of the project.

(a) Why should be undertake such interschool cooperative research project? Firstly it will be possible to have better academic inputs if we involve teachers from other schools also. Moreover, in case of bigger projects of applied research it would be possible to carry out such projects which require involvement of more teachers.

(b) In certain projects more comprehensive or bigger sample is to be drawn for more reliable results. In such cases when bigger sample of students is drawn from different schools, the results or conclusion drawn would be more valid and applicable to all those schools from which sample was drawn.

(c) Another advantage is that various types of problems encountered in assessment in different schools can be analysed in terms of problems peculiar to different institutions; or problems encountered in all the participating schools. Accordingly, these may be categorized into problems, to be investigated through action research, through applied research and may be a problem which can only be investigated through fundamental research involving all the schools in a block, district or even at the state level involving some experts from agencies like S.C.E.R.T., N.C.T.E., N.C.E.R.T. or Examination Boards. Thus problems can be classified institution-wise for action research and as cooperative inter-school-wise for applied research related problems.

(d) Such inter-school cooperative research projects provide another useful purpose for comparison of inter-school students' performance as revealed in the outcomes of research. Analysis of competency-wise performance would also be indicative of the types of inadequacies in students' learning in different institutions which form the basis for improvement and comparison of instructional impact vis-à-vis teaching learning strategies.

(e) These cooperative studies or projects help to establish professional linkages among teachers of different schools and provide opportunities to share their experiences, problems they face and other issues that confronted them during practice of their school based assessment programmes. They get opportunities to exchange their views about the usage of different types of assessment practices and related problems if any. They learn to pick up new assessment practices from teachers of other schools and their past experience.

(f) One of the most cogent reasons for such inter-school projects or research studies is the development of assessment material. Development of test material, say multiple choice tests, short-answer questions and even one or two essay type questions on some selected topic or area like say, physiology or single topic say organic evolution, would provide a good study. It would reveal the quality of questions of different types, coverage of topic and the assessment objectives tested in terms of intended learning outcomes and the teachers who developed the material. Such a material when finalized can provide good comparative performance of students, when used in testing.

(g) Such a cooperative venture would lead to development of good question banks in various areas of different subjects. Moreover the missing material on different competencies is also located and developed later to up date question banks in that particular area. To begin with such cooperative question banks can be used by schools as non-confidential for better learning. Of course later on similar lines good confidential question banks in each subject, can be developed on the basis of intended learning or assessment objectives and the competencies implied therein.

(h) Interchange of assessment material among the competing schools can go a long way for establishing of performance standards among the different schools. Of course such an action task is possible only through administrators and supervisors at the district level, who can provide the needed guidance and financial support for such a venture.

(i) Research evidences therefore, can be used to improve existing practices of S.B.A. It is for the practicing teachers or the concerned principals to initiate such research projects or other studies in the form of action research or applied research, and analyse the results and on the basis of findings improve the existing conditions.

(j) Such research studies may relate to any of the following major areas of S.B.A.:

- Assessment objectives: To judge performance of students in terms of I.L.Os and competencies implied.

- Teaching learning strategies and their impact on pupils' performance
- Tools and techniques of assessment, their validity and reliability
- Attitudes and interests of teachers and students.
- Personality traits of students in terms of adjustment, cooperation etc
- Surveys; social surveys, opinion surveys, trends studies, school studies, follow up studies, case studies, content analysis, observational studies etc.

12.3 Providing *Support Material* for Encouraging Teachers for Studies

(a) *Purpose of Support Material*

It hardly needs any mention that by and large school teachers seldom take up studies and investigations besides usual class room teaching. However, if various types of support services are provided to the teachers they would definitely be able to appreciate that small studies if undertaken and results analysed and utilized would surely help in improving teaching besides of course existing assessment practices. It is in this context that attempt is being made to identify such support services in the form of exemplar materials for teachers which would not only provide them the guide lines for developing and using such material for better assessment but also to initiate them into role of research for better assessment practices.

(b) Type of Exemplar Material

(i) *Related to Assessment Objectives:* In this context it is desirable to develop and provide assessment material like the exemplars given below:

- Questions based on single objective and multiple objectives
- Questions one each on different assessment objectives in hierarchical order

- Questions one each on all the competencies in order of complexity
- Questions framed to cover more than one competencies from the same and different assessment objectives.
- Examples of criterion—referenced objectives e.g. At the end of the lesson the "student will be able to rectify 8 out of 10 wrong spellings in the given para within 5 minutes." (Emphasis on mastery and improvement of achievement) Example of norm referenced approach where teaching is followed by testing and assignment of marks focus is on measurement not on improvement of achievement?

(ii) *Related to Teaching Learning Process*: Here exemplars can be provided related to assessment modes at the pre-instructional stage, instructional and post instructional phases eg.:

- Development of oral and written readiness tests on a specific unit of teaching to judge pre-requisite concepts considered necessary for students to understand the new unit being taught.
- Based on the same unit which is being taught, examples of types of questions which must be asked by teachers to involve students in teaching and use such questions for getting feedback about students' learning or during sectional recapitulation.
- Examples of questions on the same unit of teaching, to be used at post instructional stage, for home assignments to reinforce learning. Such questions must reflect testing of assessment objectives of the unit.

(iii) *Related to Summative Testing*: Here purpose is to make summative testing, like term or semester test and annual promotion test used normally in school based assessment though C.B.S.E. or other examining agencies tests, are well developed summative tests yet it is rarely that analysis of students' performance on these tests is undertaken to judge the quality of different questions. It is seldom that boards calculate the validity and reliability of these annual summative tests used for promotion purposes.

(a) Before giving idea of needed exemplars for summative testing it would be better if exemplars be provided on a selected unit and sub-unit in the form of unit test as also a module on a sub-unit of the same test.

(i) In case of a module formulation of I.L.Os., teaching learning activities and assessment of students' performance in terms of competencies listed under I.L.Os. be reflected, to provide guide lines to teachers for efficient teaching.

(ii) In case of unit tests criteria of a good unit test be written "in terms of assessment objectives, content analysis and form of questions."

- How best design to be developed indicating the criteria?
- How best blueprint be developed indicating the criteria?
- How best different forms of questions to be selected and used?
- How best marking scheme to be developed?
- How best to utilize analysis of results to improve students' achievement?

(c) For *Summative Testing*: Besides ensuring quality of design and blueprint of summative tests like the annual tests which teachers prepare for annual examination it is more important to ensure quality of questions framed which provide for better validity and reliability. It requires a lot of effort to develop quality questions of different types in terms of blue prints developed. However, I feel that exemplars of following types provided to teachers would definitely help them to ensure better validity, reliability and usability of our summative tests.

(i) *Essay Type Questions*: There is misunderstanding among paper setters that E.T.Qs. are the easiest to frame. However, research studies about their marking reveal that they are not property constructed to reflect properly the intended response which the examinees could know before answering. This is more true of extended response than restricted response variety of E.T.Qs. Therefore, it is better, rather necessary, that exemplars be supplied to teachers to guide them and appreciate the needed criteria to develop E.T.Q., which reflect the intended response the question setter wants, requiring students to use the intended mental processes for writing the answer to such questions. Support material in the form of constructing E.T.Q. along with intended marking scheme with respect to following types would be useful for teachers:

- Examples of good restricted response variety of E.T.Q. with well worked marking scheme developed and discussed with at least 10 to 20 experienced examiners.
- Examples of good quality questions of extended response E.T.Q. with workable marking scheme to be developed through open discussion of 10 to 20 experienced examiners.
- Examples of E.T.Q. testing different assessment objectives K.U.A.S. in the same question using any relevant unit of study or area of syllabus, along with functional marking scheme.

- Analysis of some central board test with response to E.T.Q., to find out the competencies tested under various objectives, along with marking scheme of a paper setter, to find out the strengths and weaknesses.
- Study of 5 years question papers set at any level by any examining agency to judge the relevance of the directional words used (Discuss, Describe etc.) and the extent of possible accuracy in marking such questions as 'Discuss the theories of organic evolution'

(ii) *Short Answer Questions*: This may also include very short answer (VSA) questions or fixed response questions.

- Study question papers of 5-10 different schools (unit test, term tests in or annual) and find out the S.A.Q. and V.S.A.Q. given their in. Study each question to see the objective tested and the competencies covered in those questions. Analyse to judge the quality of each question in terms of assessment objective.
- Based on a prescribed syllabus or a particular area of study develop quality questions of S.A. type each question testing different competencies under different objectives (K.U.A.S).
- Prepare a set of about 15 questions of V.S.A. variety each testing different assessment objective in terms of maximum number of competencies covered, one in each question. Draw your conclusion about their potentiality in terms of coverage of content and assessment objective.
- Study 5-10 questions papers set in an annual examination and application on different varieties of objective type questions (Constant alternative, multiple choice, matching type, master list, structured questions etc). Study the difficulties involved, competencies, covered and suggest the

role of different varieties in formative and summative testing.
- Take any programme conducted for orientation of teachers in assessment objectives and work out the activities to be under taken for planning, development, implementation and evaluation stages (b) in terms of school setting, inputs processes, outputs (c) indicating role of rational, formative and summative evaluation.

(d) *Development and Use of Question Banks*

- Teachers can develop non-confidential question banks in each subject by involving co-teachers and students from different schools. Purpose is to privde good assessment material for learning. Such a question bank when given to students for answering, provides good learning experience.
- Confidential question banks can be developed cooperatively by teaches from different schools and can be used in summative testing in term tests and annual examination. Analysis of students' performance would provide the teachers with specific strengths and weaknesses of students, on the basis of which teaching learning strategies can be adapted.
- Focus of this exercise is to encourage teachers to develop more valid test material for use in teaching and for assessment purpose and gather more valid and reliable evidences about students' achievement, make sound judgment, and meaningful reporting.

12.4 Determining Interests and Attitudes of Students for Better Teaching

(a) *Assessment of students' interest:* It is necessary for teachers to find out their different areas of interest, activities they are interested in, persons they like to work with, books they like, games they prefer to play etc. Depending upon the circumstances following considerations are relevant to evaluate the interests:

- Is the interest temporary or permanent? If temporary it may reflect lack of growth.
- Is the interest deep or superficial? If superficial it reflects lack of growth.
- Is the interest individual or group centred?
- Is the interest active or passive?
- Is the interest of the learner, moral or immoral?
- Is the interest conducive to democratic way of life?

For appraisal of interests we have to classify what evidences about interests show lack of growth and evidences about learner's interest that show growth.

(b) *Teachers' Role*: Following are the reasons why teachers should be concerned with 'the pupils' interest:

- Promoting desirable interest which already exists eg. reading books
- Developing new interests in students with narrow interests, coming from poor families
- Discouraging undesirable interests in students with poor interests and substitute them with desirable interests
- Developing better pupil-teacher rapport by establishing cooperative relationship with his pupils on the basis of sincere knowledge of their interest.
- Providing educational and vocational guidance on the basis of interests, work habits, personal discipline, self initiative and social adjustment of pupils

(c) *Evaluating Interest in Schools*: It involves

(i) *Who should evaluate*: It demands that pupil's ability to evaluate oneself and the ability to cooperatively evaluate matters of common concern and interest. Therefore, pupils have to gradually learn how to evaluate their own interest and in case of senior pupils along with teachers and parents are to do continuous evaluation of interests.

(ii) *When should one evaluate interest?* Teachers should evaluate, at the beginning of the year, gather evidence during process when attempt is made to promote new and desirable interests and discourage undesirable interests. Teacher should survey students' at the end of the year to determine desirable changes in interest. On special occasion like annual function or games, teachers can gather more complete information about a student or a group of students.

(iii) *What means can be adopted to evaluate interest* ? Two techniques are available for gathering evidences about pupils' interests, the standardized interest inventories and teacher made devices. Some of these are students' talks, class discussion interview, check lists, questionnaires, rating scales, anecdotal records, paired-comparison tests and interest inventories, teachers observational notes etc.

(d) *Standardised Devices*: Following are usable devices for measuring interests.

(i) *Ohio interests inventory*: Questionnaire or checklist is used by subject teachers. Pupils are asked to indicate in the given list of activities, by tick marks

L : If he likes the activity
I : If he is indifferent
D : If he dislikes the activity
O : If he would like some opportunity

(ii) *Strong Vocational interest Blank*: Against each activity or occupation mark

L : If he likes
D : Dislikes and
I : Indifferent

(iii) *Kudar Preference Record*: Inventory uses a forced choice in which a pupil checks the most and the least liked of the three possibilities as illustrated blow

- Read the story to a sick person
- Teach tricks to a dog
- Take apart a toy not working and to see how to repair it
- Read a fictional novel
- Write your experience of the Simla visit
- Work with other boys to develop an action plan

There are a number of other inventories but teacher made devices are better and easy to develop, like checklists, rating scales and observation. Moreover, for proper construction, use and interpretation teachers have to take help of experienced evaluators for analysis, judgmenting and identifying the desirable and undesirable interests revealed, followed by decisions regarding new interests to be developed and undesirable interests to be discouraged.

12.5 Development and Assessment of Positive Attitudes

Attitude is a mental disposition, inclination, bias, feeling or preconceived notion about idea, persons, objects, convictions or specific personal beliefs. Cognitive attitudes relate to knowledge. Positive attitudes of students towards teachers, school, their studies, students' particular subject, or particular type of activities or a profession, does make difference not only for improvement of achievement in that subject but also for better personal and social adjustment which does contribute to cognitive as well as non-cognitive learning outcomes. For evaluation of attitudes different approaches are used.

- Students are directly asked about their likes, dislikes or indifference

To indicate their preference two important techniques used are: Method of equal appearing intervals and the Lickert method.

(a) *Method of Equal Appearing Intervals*: This method devised by Thurstone and Chave for measurement of attitudes is carried out by self-report methods. In one of the methods subject is presented with a list of statements expressing attitudes that vary from very favourable, to neutral to very unfavourable and subject is asked to tick mark those with which he agrees. There can be a large number of statements of attitudes towards some thing e.g. the teachers, principal, etc. Statements must vary by fine degrees from extremely favourable to extremely unfavourable. Competent judges are asked to sort out the statements into eleven piles according to the degree of opinion expressed and reproduced in random order. Subject is asked to check those statements with which he agrees. His score or attitude is based on the average scale value of those he checks.

(b) *The Lickert Method of Measuring Attitudes*: In this case a number of statements of attitude towards something, which are decidedly either favourable or decidedly unfavourable are given. Each statement has usually 5 responses: S.A.—strongly agree; A—agree; U—undecided; D—disagree; S.D.—strongly disagree. The subject reacts to every statement by marking one of the 5 possible responses. Responses have weights of 5, 4, 3, 2, 1 for favourable statements and 1, 2, 3, 4, 5 for unfavourable responses. Subject's score is the sum of the weights of responses he checks. A high score indicates a highly favourable attitude and the low score indicates highly un-favourable attitudes. Sample set of statements by Lickert methods is as below:

Tick mark the one you agree with
All teachers are more interested in tuitions than teaching.
(SA—A—μ—SD)
Most of the students like to work individually.
(SA—A—μ—S.D)

One of the difficulty in attitude scales is their validity as in all self-reporting instruments. The subject can tick mark S.A. to simulate extreme attitude though he may not be really disposed of favourably. What a person agrees or disagrees with on paper is not necessarily his reflection of what he really feels or acts. There is no way of determining whether the subject is honestly expressing what he believes. Ultimate validity of attitude scores depends on how well, they correlate with action. This is why such data are of limited value for practical purposes.

(c) *Implication for Teaching Learning in S.B.A.*: Brief discussion on evaluation of learners' interests and attitudes was undertaken to initiate teachers to understand the need to study pupils' interests and attitudes in the content of teaching learning process and adapt their assessment practices accordingly. Purpose is to investigate and develop desirable interests and attitudes for better learning and social adjustments. Another purpose is to discourage undesirable interests and attitudes which may hinder cognitive and affective development of the learners. Besides teachers' own daily observations in various situations, various types of interest inventories and attitude scales are available some of which can be used by teachers in cooperation with other school teachers or even interschool projects can be developed. It is expected that by developing desirable interests and positive attitudes toward studies and school personnel, teachers can improve their teaching, learning strategies and assessment.

12.6 Using Research Based outcomes to Improve S.B.A.

(a) In this chapter first of all discussion on nature, purpose and scope of research in S.B.A. was done. It was followed by description of various types of studies and investigations relevant to the teaching-learning strategies and school based assessment. Discussion on inter-institutional cooperative research projects, relevant to improving instruction and assessment practices, were taken up. Role of examples and question banks for improving existing system of S.B.A. was highlighted. Focus on determining students' interest in various types of activities and their attitudes towards, various personnel, situations and teachers was considered necessary, to identify desirable and undesirable attitudes and interest. How best to utilize these findings for improving S.B.A. practices was the focal point.

(b) As a result of such studies, investigations and research projects the resultant outcomes that accrue can be utilized for working out the scientific basis to improve the existing practices. Such empirical evidences collected from various researches or studies do provide guidelines to improve the existing S.B.A. practices as mentioned below.

(i) Such investigation or research studies help to indicate the areas modes of assessment and assessment tools which need to be improved or completely dispensed with and replaced by new practices.

(ii) Identifying the causes of poor performance as well as the adequacies in the system of S.B.A. This helps the teachers to undertake remedial instruction in those areas and adapt instructional strategies for better teaching and better assessment of pupils.

(iii) Another advantage of the research outcomes is the evidences about inter-institutional studies on the basis of which the teachers can decide as to how best to undertake certain inter-institutional cooperative projects for better academic inputs to yield better academic out puts through improved S.B.A. system.

(iv) Keeping in view the limited research experience of teachers it is indeed very useful to provide good exemplars related to guidance needed in specific areas where in they don't have sufficient experience and cannot give intended inputs. It may relate to certain aspects of development or assessment, modes and assessment devices or various types of tests or test items. In a way it would provide indirect guidance to teachers for improving existing pattern of school based assessment.

(v) Use of good *question banks* is another significant resultant outcome which can profitably be used for improving assessment tools and make S.B.A. technically more valid, reliable and usable system besides improving teaching learning strategies in the context of improving formative and summative tests. In case of non-confidential question banks students involvement, and co teachers from same school or even from other schools can help in developing such question banks. Such non-confidential question banks help students to learn better because of their role in developing questions based on all testable competencies under various assessment objectives. It is assumed that such question banks are developed in the context of prescribed syllabus, textbooks and pool of questions gathered from previous question papers set during formative or summative testing. However in case of confidential question banks, only standardized tests and other terminal tests which are not publicised are to used for which subject teachers from different institutions can be involved. Use of questions from such question banks by teachers in school based assessment objectives besides setting and judging students' performance standard thereby leading to improving quality of S.B.A.

(c) *Validation of S.B.A. Practices* : Research studies outcomes would show whether these outcomes support some of the existing SBA practices and thereby validate such practices in terms of their relevance and appropriateness. On the other hand some practices may prove to be inappropriate in terms of research outcomes. Such practices which prove otherwise need to be discouraged or dispensed with it requires rethinking and review to make some practices more relevant by introducing some changes in view of research outcomes. Therefore, some changes may have to be introduced keeping in view the research findings or investigations made by teachers. Such evidences collected form various sources or research projects carried out by teachers would help to validate or invalidate some of the existing S.B.A. practices already in use.

To Sum Up

It is obvious that role of research is important to investigate the relevance and reliability of the existing practices the teachers are undertaking, in terms of aspects of assessments, modes of assessment, devices of assessment and quality of assessment tools. If necessary changes are made on the basis of research outcomes. This not only validates the existing practices by confirming or rejecting some of the existing practices but also help to further improve the system of school based assessment. Such an attempt of using research out comes for validation purpose and improving the existing practices of S.B.A. must be appreciated. It would help not only in validating existing practices of assessing pupils but would also provide leading guidelines to improve instructional practices if research outcomes are used properly.

13

Where Do We Fail in School Based Assessment?

Ever since the dawn of India's independence significant improvement in the system of education and quality of education have taken place. In the area of examinations, more particularly, the public examinations, concrete steps have been taken by National Council of Educational Research and Training (NCERT) at the national level and by Boards of School Education at the state level. It is indeed the area where maximum inputs are made to make examinations more valid and reliable measure of pupils' achievement. We have no doubt succeeded to an appreciable extent in this regard by improving the quality of paper setting, developing more detailed marking schemes, ensuring more scoring objectivity and computerization of results. Despite these perceptible reforms and other measures taken by different examining agencies, are we in a position to say that with improved examinations there are now less malpractices in conduct of examinations; they have positive impact on teaching learning practices; they no longer dictate the curricula and we have reduced the gap of performance standard of pupils from different states ? The answer is most probably not in the affirmative. Reform in public examinations by and large are undertaken in isolation from the school context and in one direction only, with emphasis on improvement of measurement value of public examinations serving mainly the judgemental function.

Examinations as a means of quality control in education can better be appreciated when evaluation becomes an integral part of the teaching learning process by serving mainly the diagnostic function. This can only be possible if Continuous Comprehensive Assessment (CCA) by teachers is an integral part of their instruction. Moreover, assessment of the whole child in a given context of school environment, is possible only through internal School-Based Assessment (SBA) carried out by school teachers themselves. It is in this background that role of SBA is now increasingly appreciated. Consider assessment and evaluation as a total school concept thereby emphasizing the inevitability of teacher based assessment of the whole child for diagnosing his inadequacies in learning to improve his achievement.

Compared to summative evaluation carried out by external examinations the School Based Assessment (SBA) is a much more potent and cogent device which aims at using assessment

(a) as an integral part of teaching and learning.
(b) for diagnostic purpose to improve instruction and pupils' learning.
(c) to maintain desired standard of performance.
(d) to provide opportunity for school self evaluation.
(e) for making sound judgements about the learner's total development and
(f) to take timely decisions to improve learners, instruction and school environments.

Thus words like continuity, integration, diagnosis, comprehensiveness, cooperativeness, quality control, feedback and improvement are the key concepts underlying philosophy of CCA.

Inspite of such a sound theoretical framework, wherever CCA is introduced in India or elsewhere, it could not succeed as an alternative to external examinations. It has failed to yield the intended dividends. In India, Rajasthan experiment of CCA where maximum possible inputs were provided both by NCERT and the Rajasthan Board, the results were not encouraging. Tamil Nadu and Kerala experiences were no better. Even in foreign countries experiences of success vary from a moderate to the least effective as revealed in a review of international perspective by the author (1993). If this is the position then where do we fail ? My own analysis of experience in the field of SBA prompts me to make some assertions relating to different aspects of CCA as to why teacher based continuous comprehensive assessment fail.

13.1 Inconsistency in Belief and Practice of S.B.A.

(a) *Historical Facts*

All documents and reports of expert committees like University Education Commission (1948), Secondary Education Commission report (1952), Kothari Commission report (1966), Ayia report (1972), NCERT 10 year scheme of schooling (1975), National Policy of Education (1986), National Curriculum framework of NCERT (1988), the report of the Ministry of Human Resource Development Government of India on Minimum Levels of Learning at the Primary Stage (1991) and onward upto the latest curriculum framework of NCERT (2005) have all highlighted the need for more valid teacher assessments by establishing sound system of continuous comprehensive assessment in schools. No one can deny that this is the only alternative to complement the record of pupils' achievement in external examinations for making certification of achievement more meaningful for admissions, selections and employment. However, more often than not school-based assessments are moderated against achievement scores on external examinations which are always criticised for their low reliability and limited assessment of the whole child. We believe CCA as a more credible mode of assessment but regard teachers' assessment less dependable.

(b) *Teachers' Predicament*

CCA is based on the fundamental concept of having faith and recognizing teachers' competence. When we introduce CCA in our schools, we have to believe and trust them as real agent of reform. In practice however, we openly blame them for subjective marking (which indeed is the objective of valid assessments). We trust them but not their assessments (in practice) and blame them for their biased outlook and partial judgements. At present some boards trust them up to 20 per cent, 25 per cent or 30 per cent and none upto 100 per cent. Accordingly 20 per cent or 25 per cent or 30 per cent weightage is given to internal assessment. We eulogise teachers' role in CCA but don't trust them fully. What a contradiction !

(c) *Total Development of Learners*

No system of SBA is worth the name if need for assessment of the whole child is not appreciated because it is only through teachers' assessment that non-cognitive outcomes of learning can be reliably tested. Inspite of that quite often we do not include in our system of CCA, assessment of non-scholastic aspects and limit it to recording of results of periodical tests and other cognitive outcomes which are easily assessed through written tests. It is one thing to believe in total development of the pupils and it is another policy to ignore assessment of non-scholastic aspects which are more difficult to assess.

(d) *Diagnostic Purpose Undermined*

It hardly needs any mention that focus of SBA is on diagnosis of pupils' learning difficulties and improving their achievement through remedial measures. In actual practice unit tests and other periodical tests are used more for grading and certification of pupils' achievement than for diagnosis and remediation, thereby defeating the very purpose of continuous assessment. This gap in theory and practice mitigates the purpose of CCA.

(e) *Illuminative Approach*

SBA envisages preference for descriptive and illuminative approach using tests, teachers' observations, peer evaluation and parents' opinion for collecting and meaningful reporting of evidences about pupils' attainments. In practice, however, application of psychometric methods are considered more appropriate for interpretation and reporting of performance.

The question is which of the two approaches is in line with the philosophy of SBA?

(f) ***Criterion Referencing in Testing***

Though criterion-referenced measurement is emphasized in SBA to encourage testing for mastery learning thereby improving performance levels of pupils yet the performance of pupils is judged in terms of norm referenced measure and pass a pupil at 30, 33 or 35 per cent marks keeping the average pupil as focus of testing. Interpretation of marks in terms of variation from the norm or class performance rather than the criteria of mastery, still remains the yard stick of comparison.

From the foregoing analysis of what is accepted and what is practiced we are in a position to see the stark reality of dichotomous thinking of the decision makers and other stake holders. They apparently believe in the philosophy of SBA but are not prepared to shed off the existing practices which are incompatible with that philosophy. Therefore my first assertion is:

> *No sound system of SBA can be established successfully unless its protagonists develop firm conviction and unfailing belief in their teachers' assessments. And for that the first and the foremost condition is that the above mentioned dichotomies observable in theory and practice must be conceptualised by the decision makers.*

13.2 Unrealistic Planning and Inadequate Preparation

(1) ***Unrealistic Planning***

(a) *Cognizance of Objectives of SBA*: If the objectives of SBA in terms of intended outcomes are not clearly formulated and stated in testable form, action tasks related to those objectives of reform cannot be properly identified. Ambitious planning, howsoever meticulous it may be is bound to fail if objectives and targets are not realistic in terms of resources and inputs available. Later on it will neither be possible to withdraw some of the objectives nor undertake reformulation of action tasks once the implementation of the scheme starts.

(b) *Capacity Building*: Introduction of CCA in schools involves a lot of financial and human resource inputs. It is in such a project that demands all the year round attention of the practitioners of reform and those of the stake holders in the project. On the basis of appraisal of existing resources and project budget intended goals are set and time targetted. Availability of human resources and the capacity building potential of the school board and directorate of education would determine the functionality of the programme budget and fixing of long range and short range targets to be achieved.

(c) *Sustainability of Reform*: High sounding objectives, unrealistic targets and ambitious programme budget would require involvement of unmanageable army of workers for developing execution, monitoring and evaluating the programmes for which quite heavy infrastructure would be needed. It would lead to more problems and challenges that would be difficult to meet. Intended dividends would not be accrue and it would not be possible to sustain the on-going reform.

(d) *Need Assessment Strategy*: Unless need assessment, through survey of existing practices of SBA, is undertaken it will not be possible to work out the mode of introducing reform. Whether intensive work in selected schools is to be the model on pilot basis to be preferred or an extensive coverage of all schools in the state is to be the mode of implementation ? Will it be possible to provide differential inputs in different schools depending upon the state of art in each school? Accordingly, decision is taken whether metamorphic changes are to be introduced or incremental doses of reform are to be given to each school. Decision about implementation model has therefore, to be taken by the board in view of the likely impact it will have on improvement of school programmes and the collateral effects that it would engender.

(e) *Portfolio of Evidences and Resource Material*: It is again during planning stage that sometimes we decide to encompass an impracticable portfolio of evidences in our system of S.B.A. and we fail to implement. Record of achievement on scholastic aspects of pupils' attainment, collection of evidences on affective development of pupils, gathering information about pupils' psychomotor outcomes of learning and recording of teacher's observations about personal social qualities of pupils, is not an easy job for every teacher. It demands construction and application of various tools and techniques of assessment besides keeping regular, systematic and comprehensive record of achievement. It requires development of different proformas and keeping regular record of each aspect of pupils' growth and attainments involving a lot of registration work. Not only that, it is a cumbersome job to collate different types of evidences in the form of pupils' profiles' for meaningful reporting and certification of achievement. Introduction of ambitious portfolio of evidences may ultimately lead to undesirable collateral effects like fake records of achievement, fictitious data, entries, etc.

It is at the planning stage that acquaintance with prevailing assessment practices, assessment of needs, identification of task in relation to objectives of reform, taking stock of resources and introduction of manageable portfolio of evidences is essential before we start preparing ourselves for the reform. In this context I make my second assertion as follows:

If the objectives of SBA are not realistically formulated and properly time targeted, in terms of specific outcomes, keeping in view the financial resources available and the capacity building potential for human resource development, it would not be possible to establish successfully the proposed pattern of school-based assessment.

(2) *Inadequate Preparation*

(a) *Policy Statement*: If the planning is meticulous and realistic next step is to get set and be ready for interventions and innovations to be introduced. Making haste, without needed readiness, will result in haphazard implementation and unintended collateral effects. It is, therefore, necessary that the policy statement on introduction of reform must be formulated and stated in advance highlighting the need for introduction of SBA objectives of reform, significant components of improvement, strategy to be adopted; personnel to be involved and mode of evaluating the programme effects.

(b) *Theoretical Framework*: Need for *Growth Oriented Model*: It is assumed that the scheme being launched is based on a pedagogically sound theoretical model that is indigenously developed and rooted in its native soil rather than an imported foreign model of developed countries which is bound to fail. What is needed, is the growth oriented model suited to the genius of a democratic, socialistic, developing country like India or Mauritius. One such model recently worked out at Mauritius Examinations Syndicate and discussed at the 19th meeting of the International Association of Educational Assessment (1993) was ready for launching. Without a sound theoretical framework, a scheme can neither be justified nor can be properly dove tailed in a given system of education to ensure the intended outputs.

(c) *Linkages with Allied Agencies*: A good educational system works in a given social milieu of which it is a part. No scheme howsoever, meticulously planned, can operate effectively without the continual support and cooperation of the allied educational agencies in the state. For additional inputs, dynamic interaction for sustaining reform and capacity building of institutions, need for ensuring proper linkages with agencies like

SCERT, teacher training colleges, university departments of education, DIETS and Directorates of Education cannot be over-emphasised at this stage and also during implementation stage. Close collaboration of these agencies can be sought by associating their experts or representatives with advisory committees, steering committees, implementation committees and evaluation committees. This linkage would prevent an unwarranted criticism and bottle-necks in the implementation of the scheme. Do we establish such linkages ?

(d) *Social Climate for Acceptability of Reform*: Creation of conducive social climate is essential for acceptability of the reform in the field. Therefore, sensitization of the public in general and the practitioners of reform in particular, is the precursor for launching the project of SBA. This can be done through mass media like newspapers, television and radio besides publicity through posters, brochures, pamphlets and monographs. Community acceptance can be assured through meetings of Parent Teacher Associations and inviting experts from community for associating them in various committees for the decision taking processes. If this is done community will not only accept but even support and accelerate the pace of reform by owning the project. But how many projects seek such support to create social climate, is anybody's guess.

(e) *Training Packages for Staff Development*: Another important thing at preparatory stage is to develop training packages for training of key persons who would act as resource persons for orientation of teachers and other personnel entrusted with the introduction and dissemination of reform. Such training packages would include written modules on different aspects of innovations, video tapes, exemplar material, assessment tools, etc. This would help the clientele to adopt the changes more easily besides acting as a means for staff development to improve their technical know how, thereby facilitating the implementation of reform.

(f) *Portfolios of Evidences*: At this stage cognizance has to be taken of the nature and scope of portfolio of evidences that would form the basis for certification of pupils on SBA. Accordingly, various proformas and other documents like report cards, progress report cards, cumulative record cards, etc. are to be developed and kept ready for use immediately after the reform is introduced in the schools. Once such documents relating to record of pupils' achievement are ready, training of key persons and teachers will create no problem or difficulty in introducing the reform smoothly.

Let us now take stock of the actual realities that we observe during introduction of the scheme of SBA. Do we really prepare ourselves convincingly, mentally and academically to see that right model based on a sound theoretical framework is chosen; policy document on reform with clear indicators of expected and acceptable outcomes and end-products is worked out; proper linkage with allied agencies is established; awareness among the community is developed and the training materials and record cards are developed before launching the project. I have my doubts. That quite a few such projects fail just at the launching pad before their actual take off is a stark reality. This makes me to pronounce my third assertion as under:

In the absence of a clear cut policy statement based on a sound theoretical model suited to the native soil, no amount of resource and efforts would yield the intended outputs. Even if an appropriate model is worked out it would never be possible to introduce the reform successfully, unless cooperation of allied agencies is tapped, public is duly sensitized; training packages are developed and the documents for recording pupils' attainment are kept ready in time before launching the project.

13.3 Ineffective Implementation Strategy

(a) *Participative Strategy*: In a democratic social set up like that in a of state of India, a centralised, autocratic or state imposed strategy is neither possible nor desirable to ensure needed cooperation of the clientele and collaboration of different agencies. It has to be a participative strategy for implementation of the scheme. For development of materials, training of teachers, research support, effective monitoring of reform, close interaction and involvement of all the stake holders of reform is necessary for democratic decision making processes. Therefore, it is not only the teachers but also the parents, the community, allied agencies and the pupils themselves who are to be involved if the reform is to be sustained and institutionalised properly in schools.

(b) *Involving Teachers' Union*: It is not uncommon to find that many reforms do not make much headway because teachers' unions and headmasters or principals' associations are not associated with the reform at various stages. Their expertise and views can be sought by associating their representatives on subject panels for developing materials, validation of materials and during other stages of implementation. This will ensure not only their continued support and acceptance but also keep them aware of the on-going reform and the significance of their role in implementing the scheme of SBA.

(c) *School Clusters Wise Cooperative Testing:* There is no gain saying that resources of different schools are not the same in terms of teachers' and pupils' inputs. We cannot expect all schools to progress evenly at the same pace to develop and utilize test material during implementation. It is, therefore, necessary to develop within each district, school clusters in each educational block. Depending upon the number of schools in each block mini clusters of 5 to 10 schools may be developed, which in turn form the school complex at the block level. The block level school clusters would then form the district level macro-cluster of schools. Link between mini clusters at block level can be established by a coordination committee of representatives of those schools. Likewise at district level a steering committee of block level representatives of those schools can be set up to monitor development of materials and progress of reform. Sharing of expertise and resources of different schools would accelerate the pace of reform and minimize the inter-school variations in performance assessment can be established. Can we achieve parity of performance standards in the absence of such a cooperative test development strategy, without sacrificing equity and social justice?

(d) *Multipronged Approach for Introducing Reform*: While introducing reform multipronged approach has to be adopted so that the various changes and innovations are properly institutionalized. In-service education of teachers cannot be carried on endlessly every year. Incorporation of concept and practice of SBA in the curriculum of pre-service teacher-training at B.Ed level would be necessary to make it integral part of teachers' equipment. Strategy of in-service education of teachers through development of nucleus of resource persons by intensive training of District Education Officers/ Inspectors/Supervisors/Block Education Officers would be necessary for reorientation of practitioners of reform as a part of crash programme of human resource development. Do we use this strategy ?

(e) *Mode of Dissemination of Reform*: Another important strategy is to use the most practicable and effective mode of diffusion and dissemination of reform so that changes are accepted by public, allied agencies, schools and all other stake holders of reform. For this an official organ of the Board, like a news letter, a journal or a special bulletin about the on-going reform and impact of CCA pupils' achievement can be taken advantage of. No amount of preparation will generate desired impact unless the clientele is kept aware of the positive impact and progress or reform. This leads to my fourth assertion as under:

Inspite of meticulous planning and adequate preparation, reform movement will never gain momentum and yield the intended dividends unless the reform is integrated with reform in teacher education curriculum, school-based teaching learning practices, system of certification of achievement and the role of allied educational agencies. And for that need for participative strategy of planning, developing and evaluating materials, programmes and outcomes cannot be over-emphasised.

13.4 Unplanned *Introduction of Reform*

Can we ensure that reform will be firmly rooted and established if it is planned well, with necessary preparation and appropriate strategy devised for implementation ? Not necessarily; though foundations are laid well for take off. There are quite a few decisions which are to be taken about phasing of reform, time targeting, success indicators, monitoring or reforms, in-built formative evaluation and feedback mechanism, before introducing the proposed scheme of assessment.

(a) *Phasing of Reform*: Are we going to introduce SBA in selected schools on a pilot basis for trialing to review the proposed scheme before introducing it on a mass scale in all schools? This would depend on initial financial resources and availability of human resources. If yes, in which district would you like to introduce for trialis or which blocks of a district are to be sampled? Decisions are to be taken in a view of the sampling requirements, the facilities available and human resource development potential. If it is to be introduced in the whole state at the same time then decision about mode of incremental doses of reform may have to be decided regarding area of improvement (scholastic followed by co-scholastic); tools to be used (unit tests, oral tests, teacher observations etc) and mechanics of collecting, recording and reporting of data (records, profiles/progress reports etc.)

(b) *Time Targeting*: Once decision of phasing of reform is taken long range and short range targets are to be fixed and accordingly major tasks to be set indicating the schedule of activities to be followed to accomplish each task within the time prescribed for each task. A two column calendar of activities and the corresponding time targets against each major task may be developed for teachers and education officers/inspectors to follow. This would keep them aware and conscious to strive hard for achieving the set targets by seriously following the time table of activities.

(c) *Accountability Criteria:* Unless accountability of each trustee of reform is at stake it is difficult to ensure and expect the practitioners of reform to deliver the quality goods in time. Teacher must be told the criteria or the indicators of achievement on the basis of which their performance will be judged. Inspectors or education officers must be made cognizant of the time tabling of activities and the time targets for which they would be held responsible. Directorate of education must also be accountable for providing the needed facilities, services, financial resources and development of human resources. Unless clear cut indicators, worked out by experts for all the practitioners, of reform are formulated, their accountability cannot be built in.

(d) *Project In-built Evaluation*: No project can succeed or yield expected results if its protagonists remain oblivious of the enroute products, materials, outcomes, difficulties, constraints and unintended effects, while the project is in progress. Therefore, formative evaluation has to be in-built in the project to get regular feedback for adjusting or adapting the implementation strategy and the time tabling of activities as also the inputs. It might also give clue to the need for some investigations to corroborate some outputs and provide correctives if needed.

(e) *Monitoring, Evaluation and Feedback*: Obviously monitoring of reform in schools has to be centralized and carried out by the school board through the agency of education officers/supervisors/inspectors. This involves activities like scheduling and time targeting of programmes; providing needed inputs and services; removing regional or institutional imbalances of inputs; coordination of different agencies; undertaking summative evaluation of programmes and institutions. Need for applying quality control measures like use of common term tests, diagnostic tests and even annual examinations, establishment of teachers question banks etc cannot be undermined.

Are you sure that all schemes of CCA are introduced and monitored with all the above mentioned pre-requisites ? If not, can we succeed with half hearted attempts ? This initiates me to make my fifth assertion as under:

No scheme of SBA can be successfully introduced in a given system of education unless its implementation is properly phased out, laying realistic time targets for the accomplishment of various tasks with in-built mechanism of formative evaluation in terms of accountability criteria and systematically monitored for providing feedback on inputs, processes and outcomes for the decision makers.

13.5 Insufficient Support Services

(a) *Sustainability Factors*: When the reform is introduced it has to be sustained by means of a number of support services that provide for motivation of teachers, reinforcement of innovations and follow up work. Some schemes of reform continue as long as project is in progress and then go down the drain losing its impact. Unless we take care of sustainability factors it is difficult to keep the on-going reform at the same pitch. Lack of supply of test material would make it impossible for teachers to construct good tools of assessment. Small brochures on exemplar material in the form of unit tests prepared by NCERT, SCERT,

DIET, etc could improve the situation. Encouraging establishment of teachers' question banks in schools would act as quality control device for development of unit tests, term tests and annual examinations.

(b) *Feedback Services*: Inadequate provision of technical services by the boards also lowers the sustainability of reform. Therefore, feeding the schools with relevant literature in the form of newsletters, bulletins, handouts, video tapes, teacher meets, etc can be of great help in sustaining the reform. Neglecting reorientation of teachers for sustaining the reform, lack of needed community support and parent teachers' associations also leads to the demotivation of teachers. Thus, it is necessary to continue contact for keeping them informed about the progress of work and the outcomes of their efforts. Their role should be appreciated in such meetings, to eulogise their association with the project.

(c) *Disseminating Reform*: Poor dissemination of outputs of reform also lowers the acceptability of public since they remain ignorant of what exactly is the reform about or its impact. Therefore, full advantage may be taken to publicise the relevance, significance and likely impact of the project through mass media like TV, radio, news papers as well as through printed pamphlets, leaflets, booklets, news bulletins, video tapes, teacher meets, etc.

(d) *Linkages with Allied Agencies*: If the linkage with allied agencies is ineffective it is bound to affect the sustainability of reform. All the collaborating agencies must not remain on paper only but their close interaction and participation is necessary to vitalize and dynamise the reform movement. An advisory committee representing these agencies can generate the needed support.

(e) *Research Support*: It is seldom that research support is provided to the on-going reform as it requires, technical competence, more time and some financial help to undertake functional and action research, findings of which can support the reform by incorporating them to improve the situation. Some class based actual problems relating to School-Based Assessment can be identified by those who monitor the reform undertaken by staff of local educational agencies and the practising teachers. This would not only sustain reform but would also lead to staff development.

History of various innovations and reforms introduced would reveal that only in exceptional cases care has been taken to provide all the above mentioned support services to enrich and sustain reforms visualized in a project. How long such a scheme can prolong its starvation death in the absence of these support services? In this context I am forced to make my sixth assertion as under:

Even a successful scheme of SBA would ultimately degenerate into a caricature if provision for supportive services like regular supply of test material, augmentation of feedback services, establishing linkage with allied agencies, dissemination of reform impact and use of functional research is not made to sustain the on-going reform in School-Based Assessment.

13.6 Unrealistic Summative Evaluation

Last stage of a project on SBA is obviously the summative evaluation of the scheme with a view to renew the same by adjusting the ends and the means. Failure of a project means that the objectives of the scheme of SBA formulated earlier at the planning stage, have not been achieved to the desired extent. A comprehensive appraisal is warranted and it has to be school specific.

(a) *Outcome Evaluation*: More often the sponsors judge the reliability of continuous assessment against pupils' performance on a common public examination conducted by the school boards. The difference in mean achievement scores on written external examination, is taken as indicator of the comparative performance of pupils from different schools. This appraisal has little validity because the objectives of SBA relate to total development of pupils unlike that of external examinations which are limited to testing of only measurable scholastic aspects. Moreover, judging outcomes of teacher based assessment against the external examinations whose reliability is often questioned, cannot be justified since the criterion used for judgement is itself not tenable and does not meet the requisite criteria of the criterion used. It is, therefore, unfair to judge the efficacy of the scheme only in terms of pupils' scholastic achievement.

(b) *Contextual Evaluation*: When we emphasise SBA as school specific, each with its own strengths, limitations, setting and learning environment, how would the limited evidences offset the effects of school context on the basis of single examination results? In a given context, pupils may demonstrate better disposition of attitudes, interests and values than cognitive development due to more community involvement and organization of interesting programmes and co-curricular activities. A school located in a backward remote area of the state with poor infra-structure and facilities would have limited impact on pupils' cognitive and social development. Therefore, need for context evaluation cannot be put aside while evaluating the outputs of SBA in a school.

(c) *Input and Process Evaluation*: Each school has differential inputs in terms of financial and human resources. Teachers' qualifications, pupils' intake, teaching learning strategies, quality of test material developed, assignments used, co-curricular activities undertaken, facilities and services provided, etc. are all relevant components of assessment for input evaluation. Unless outcomes are judged in terms of availability and utilization of inputs, the evidences that accrue cannot be relied upon for forming right judgements. In view of differential inputs and varied instructional and implementation strategies both input and process evaluation are necessary if we are keen to pass sound judgements about effectiveness of the scheme.

(d) Impact Evaluation: A good programme of SBA may result in positive impact on community and ensure much better cooperation, involvement and support-services in running the school. It may result in unintended or collateral effects like biased outlook among teachers, lenient marking, positive attitude towards internal assessment, whole some interests in pupils, professional growth of teachers etc. Thus summative evaluation must also encompass the area of impact evaluation, otherwise it will not be comprehensive evaluation and may lead to wrong inferences.

(e) *School Self-Evaluation*: There is hardly any exaggeration in saying that SBA is a total school concept and encompasses pupils' attainments, teacher development, instructional efficiency, effectiveness of implementation strategy, material assessment, programme appraisal and impact on school practices. Therefore, evaluation of the whole child in a given school environment in terms of its context, inputs, processes and outputs is necessary to identify the real strengths and weaknesses on the basis of which steps are to be taken to find relevant solutions to the emergent problems. Unless a thorough school self-evaluation is undertaken annually involving school personnel, community and other stake holders of reform, proper revitalistion of the scheme would neither be possible nor desirable to achieve the reformulated summative objectives.

(f) *Renewal of the Scheme*: On the basis of summative evaluation, school self-evaluation and follow up studies undertaken, findings should be feedback to schools with suggestions for improvement. Implementation strategy may also need modification to institutionalize the reform hereby leading to redevelopment of action plan in the light of experience, outcome evaluation and findings of the research undertaken. Renewal of the scheme may then also require some significant changes in allied areas like curriculum development, teacher training, development of textual material, mode of formative assessment and certification of pupils' achievement. With the redevelopment of the scheme of CCA action plan has also to be reviewed before launching the second phase of reform with more practical insight into the achievable goals, time targeting, programme budgeting and effective strategy of implementing the scheme.

Do we really undertake annual school self-evaluation in terms of its own context or setting, resource inputs, programmes, outcomes and programme effects? Perhaps, never; it is usually incomplete and inadequate, thereby reflecting much less valid evidences than required. And it is unprofessional and unethical also to draw conclusions on the basis of such limited data, that we use to pass off-the-cuff judgements on pupils, teachers and schools and take decisions for renewal of the scheme of S.B.A. I would, therefore, make my seventh assertion as under:

Even if the scheme of SBA is successfully implemented an unscientific summative evaluation would lead to wrong inferences, unjustified judgments and ultimately unwarranted decisions about modifications to renew the action plan, unless thorough summative evaluation and school self-evaluation are undertaken using not only pupil evaluation but also context evaluation, input evaluation process evaluation, product evaluation and impact evaluation of the project.

To Conclude

Establishing a sound system of School Based Assessment in schools is the only alternative to improve validity of existing assessment procedures used to certify pupils' achievement. The more comprehensive and continuous the assessment the more valid and reliable evidences would accrue about total growth and development of pupils, both in cognitive and non-cognitive domain. To ensure such evidences we have to depend entirely, not partially on the competence, integrity and goodwill of the teacher. he must be fully convinced that we would have complete faith in him and depend on him to implement the scheme, for which cooperation of all administrators and other decision makers would be readily forth coming at all stages of reform. Once we are assured we must not only believe teachers but also in their assessments. Teachers would never fail us provided the trustees and stake holders of reform themselves develop firm conviction and faith in the teacher assessments and shed off dichotomous role of appreciating SBA in theory but disbelieve in practice by allowing moderation of their assessment against those very external public examinations reliability of which we always decry.

Develop an indigenous growth oriented, academically sound and workable model with the help of teachers, which suits the niche in which it is to grow and fructify. Any foreign model if implemented in native soil would never develop or yield the expected dividends. If the planning is done on the basis of need assessment, resources available and collaborating agencies, it facilitates time targeting of tasks, programme budgeting, mode of introduction, nature of portfolio evidence required for certification, etc. to make it cost effective. Inadequate preparation for launching the project would result in chaos unless all relevant measures are taken in the form of policy statement, theoretical framework, cooperation of collaborating agencies, sensitization of public, development of training packages and recording documents, besides tapping of financial resources. Reform will not go very far and cannot be implemented if the participative strategy is not adopted.

Decisions about phasing of reform, accountability criteria, in built formative evaluation, centralised monitoring, regular feedback to schools and in-service orientation of personnel are to be taken for effective implementation. Untimely introduction of reform might cause some unforeseen problems. If it goes with the onset of an educational plan like renewal of curriculum, changes in pattern of external examinations, teacher training progrmmes, etc. it can be integrated with overall master plan of educational development. Lack of support services, effect the sustainability of reform for which supply of test material, encouraging teachers' question banks, provision of technical services, continued community support, linkage with related agencies and research support are necessary. Need for summative evaluation in accordance with school setting, resource inputs, instructional interventions, pupils' attainment and impact on instructional and evaluation practices, cannot be over-emphasised for review and renewal of the scheme on the basis of experience, outcome evaluation and follow up studies.

Thus establishing a sound system of School Based Assessment in Schools of a state is very demanding. It requires cooperative planning, continual vigil and attention, timely replenishment of resources, redevelopment of action tasks, adaption of implementation strategy, phases introduction of innovations, appraisal of enroute and products for feedback and correctives, seeking full collaboration of allied agencies, reorientation of personnel, reinforcement of support services and end of the term (or session) comprehensive school-evaluation. This is necessary for diagnosing strengths and weaknesses in operational strategy curriculum transactions by teachers and programme effects on the basis of which the scheme can be reviewed and action plan redeveloped. The fact is that administrators are not able to conceptualise the dichotomy of their belief and practice; do not undertake cooperative planning of projects; do not develop indigenous pedagogical model of SBA, make insufficient preparation before launching the scheme; rarely use participative strategy of implementation, do not set realistic time targets, no cooperative test development is undertaken and reasonable inputs from other agencies are not ensured. Summative evaluation is not school specific and above all research support is always lacking. That is why more often than not we fail to institutionalise successfully the scheme of Continuous Comprehensive Assessment vis-à-vis School Based Assessment. And this is the stark reality which no one can deny in Indian context.

14

Crucial Emerging Practical Issues

14.1 How Best to Make Scheme Acceptable?

(a) *It should be administratively feasible/functional*

(i) Howsoever good scheme of S.B.A. may be unless it is possible to administer it successfully in the class room situation it is of no use. Functionally it should be possible for all teachers to implement it effectively in the existing conditions. It should neither be too comprehensive nor too unmanageable by most of the teachers. It should not be so complicated and time consuming that it affects adversely the teaching learning process.

(ii) It should also be not too technical to be practiced by an average teacher. Technically it may require orientation of teachers for putting it into practice but should not involve theoretically high level of measurement theory and specialisation which makes it difficult for teachers to put into practice to the desired extent.

(iii) It should involve reasonable extent of record keeping which is practicable and consumes reasonable time in up-keeping. An unnecessary cumbersome record keeping makes it impractical as well as unnecessary. It may be usable with ease of administration in all schools, not only top class public schools.

(b) *Scheme of S.B.A. should be professionally tenable*

(i) System of S.B.A. must be based on sound theoretical principles of measurement and assessment to up keep reliability of students' assessment as well as relevance of assessment.

(ii) All modes of assessment and methodology adopted for assessment should be in tune with the educational objectives and reflected in the teaching learning processes or curriculum prescription ie assessment objectives should be geared to the prescribed curriculum objectives.

(iii) Focus of measurement should remain on testing holistic development of learners so that proper judgments could be made about the learners' growth.

(c) *Scheme of S.B.A. must be publically acceptable*

When it is decided that scheme of S.B.A. is to be given 20 per cent, 25 per cent or more weightage in the system of certification of students' achievement it must be acceptable by parents, public in general and in fact by all the stake holders of reform to make it more genuine and trustworthy. There are various ways and means which can be adopted to make the scheme publically accepted as under:

(i) It has to be highlighted that but for S.B.A. system holistic development vis-à-vis assessment of learners will not be possible. Moreover, issue of a separate certificate of internal assessment under the board's certificate would further convince the public of the validity's of the certificate issued to students.

(ii) Regular involvement of community and parent teachers association in various decision taking processes related to S.B.A. would further make them convinced about the need of S.B.A. system.

(iii) Regular feedback of good outputs of SBA in the form of good learning or students' involvement would further strengthen the role of S.B.A. Use of new assessment devices used in S.B.A. be published in news quarterly magazines or evaluation journal and get opinion and suggestions on devices used, from different agencies like SCERTs, Boards, NCERT etc.

(iv) Getting students' opinion on assessment devices and used to seek positive opinion of students about S.B.A., which may be sent to parents, community and related educational agencies.

(v) Organize public meetings cooperatively by 5 to 10 schools to convey about improved system of SBA being used and get public reflections.

(d) S.B.A. system must be legally defensible

(i) Every system of S.B.A. should be free from any legal implication. It has to be high lighted that but for teachers' assessment no system can be more authentic.

(ii) How maximum objectivity is being ensured and subjectivity reduced to minimum which indeed is the right of the teachers who teach.

(iii) Moreover, it has also to be ensured that students are given chance to improve their achievement and they are not being labelled as under achievers.

(iv) It has to be further highlighted that focus of teachers' assessment (S.B.A.) is not only on measuring students' achievement as in case of Boards' examination and even annual examination, purpose being on grading, but focus of SBA is on improvement of students' achievement.

(e) *SBA should be economically viable*

It is obvious that SBA system is an integral part of teaching learning process. Except for formal pre-announced unit tests or term tests, SBA is integrated with instructional processes. Special payment to teachers for setting, conducting and examining pupils' scripts is not warranted and neither it is time targetted for assessing students during the sessions. Likewise no printing charges for setting a question paper or for organizing other assessment activities. Of course usual expenditure on various examination processes would be there and attempt should be made to make SBA functional, efficient and cost effective.

14.2 How Best to Minimise Teachers' Subjectivity in Assessment?

(a) The most significant criticism about introduction of internal assessment in schools is the subjective assessment of teachers. In fact it should be appreciated that the subjectivity of teachers in assessing their students is indeed their right since it is they alone who know their wards the most in terms of their learning. S.B.A. assumes that teacher who teaches has the right to assess his wards and is the most appropriate person to evaluate them and certify their achievement.

(b) However, most often it is observed that some teachers are lenient and others are strict in marking which lead to leniency error or severity error of measurement. It is these types of errors which affect students' score and make it non-comparable among students from different teachers from the same and different institutions. The more objective assessment devices are used the less subjectivity would be in marking.

(c) Use of common methodology of using same assessment objectives, content elements in a given unit of study, modes of assessment, tools of assessment development of marking scheme, proper scheduling of time tabling and conduct of tests or examinations do improve validity and reliability of teachers' S.B.A. and lead to better comparability of inter-school students' performance.

(d) To reduce further and minimize subjectivity in marking, steps like the following can be taken by the class teachers.

- Using right type of questions to ensure in built scoring objectivity
- Using short answer questions requiring fixed response e.g.
    - (i) Describe four properties of carbon dioxide (more subjective marking)
    - (ii) Give two examples, one each of an aquatic plant and a desert plant (better)

(iii) List two chemical properties of CO_2 that differ form that of O_2 (Better)

(e) Use proper directional word to pin point intended response as in (ii).

(f) Develop marking scheme which leads to objective marking or grading. In case of short-answer open ended questions develop marking scheme with the help of co-teachers. Then get it examined by involving different teachers who examine the scripts using prescribed scheme developed by the paper setter. Discussion among examiners lead to final marking scheme.

(i) Let some of the scripts examined by second examiner from the same school to see the relevance of the marking scheme developed.

(ii) Let the students ie the examinees check their score and raise objections if in certain case there is some leniency or severity in marking or any other discrepancy which can be taken note of.

(g) *Moderation of Assessment Made*

(i) In case of open ended questions moderation of marking scheme developed by the paper setters may be undertaken especially when certain types of summative tests are being used for grading as in case of term test. Of course such a moderation should be done by the senior subject teachers (not teaching the same class) from the same school.

(ii) In case of annual examinations which are used for promotion or sometimes for certification of achievement moderation of marking scheme vis-à-vis construction of questions, be better undertaken by senior teachers from other schools or some evaluation expert in the same subject area. This would not only ensure scoring objectivity but would also improve wording of the question to ensure use of intended mental process in answering the question.

(h) *Moderation of SBA Marks Against Boards' Examination Results*: It looks strange that SBA marks be moderated against Boards examination results. Assumption is that boards examinations are accepted as more valid and reliable than S.B. assessments. Therefore, moderation against such an examination results can be justified. Of course it is assumed that moderation would be more appropriate against students' achievement on curricular subjects, rather than against total or wholistic development of learners as assessed in S.B.A. It is therefore, desirable that S.B.A. be recorded separately on students' assessment on prescribed curriculum in a subject and on non-cognitive or co-scholastics aspects. High correlation between students' score on S.B.A. (Cognitive learning outcomes) and boards achievement scores in that subject would indicate efficiency and effectiveness of instruction by the teacher. Over the years it would not only reflect teachers' instructional efficiency but also the validity and reliability of teachers S.B.A. assessment.

(i) *Use of question banks to minimize subjectivity in assessment*: It is quite obvious that if objective type questions of multiple choice type of or any other variety, are made use of frequently in S.B.A. it would ensure 100 per cent scoring objectivity without involving any subjective assessment. As suggested earlier development and use of non-confidential question banks with the help of students are equally good and are quite valid for assessment without involving any subjectivity in marking. Likewise, other well developed confidential question banks by teachers, examining agencies or other educational agencies, if used for summative evaluation would almost do away with subjective assessment of class teachers? Focus of this reform in minimizing subjectivity in marking is to trust teachers for their assessment and make S.B.A. more reliable and a practical reality.

14.3 How Best to Moderate Teachers' Assessment?

(a) *Why to Moderate Teachers' Assessment?*

As discussed in the last subsection on minimizing subjectivity in teachers assessment need for moderation of teachers' assessment cannot be over-emphasised. Moderation can be undertaken at three levels.

(i) Moderation of subject-wise assessment is needed to offset tendency of some teachers to be lenient in marking or assessing their students and of some teachers to be strict in marking there by making either leniency or severity errors of measurement.

(ii) Moderation of intra-school and inter-subject assessment made by different teachers is necessary to avoid unfair comparison of marks in different subjects especially when different subjects are taught by different teachers, besides varying difficulty levels of question papers set by different teachers.

(iii) Moderation of inter-school subject-wise assessment to bring some parity of intended learning outcomes and expected performance standard. Purpose is minimize variation in grading pattern and marking pattern for better comparative view of inter-school students' performance on assessment objectives and marking scheme remaining the same.

(b) *When to Moderate Students' Assessment?*

(i) After each unit of teaching when unit test is administered and scored, the students may be returned their answer scripts and asked to go through and point out discrepancy if any which may be rectified by the teacher.

(ii) After each term test which is just like quarterly examination covering about one fourth of the course. Since quarterly test are usually summative tests unlike unit tests, students scores on term tests carry more weightage in final assessment and therefore, moderation of learners' assessment in such tests.

(iii) After each annual test conducted by the school used for promotion, and certification of students' achievement and therefore, has to be more dependable, reducing the measurement errors to the maximum to make it more usable for comparison of intra-school and inter-school students' performance in all the subjects. Being the most comprehensive test its validity and reliability has to be ensured maximally.

(c) ***Levels at which to Moderate?***

(i) *Moderation at teachers level*: Class teacher who teaches can moderate his own assessment made during formative evaluation focus of which is on improvement of students learning and his own instruction. Here review of grading, peer evaluation or group based moderation through students' opinion are possible ways.

(ii) *Moderation at co-teachers' level*: In case of unit tests grading by the class teachers of his wards can be got moderated by co-teachers teaching the same subject to another section of the same class. This would ensure better parity of standard of assessment by different teachers teaching the same subject.

(iii) *Moderation of assessment at inter-school level*: If possible and acceptable, at least annual examination results of a school be moderated by teachers from different school. This would better set comparability of students' standards. Moreover, it would ensure exchange of ideas on setting papers and mode of moderation.

(iv) *Moderation against performance in Boards examination*: It is desirable to synchronize teacher based school assessment with marking and grading reflected in the board examination (For further details see 14.2 described earlier).

(d) ***Who should Moderate?***

- Moderation of unit test assessment can best be made by co-teacher teaching the same class but different section.

- Moderation of the term tests assessment by senior co-teachers form the same school teaching higher classes.
- Moderation of annual question papers and marking schemes may be undertaken cooperatively be a team of three teachers from different schools for better assessment and sharing of experience and problems.
- Moderation by departmental subject specialist supervisors who can also ensure more valid and usable mode of assessment in different schools.

(e) *How to Moderate Assessments?*

(i) Moderation against board examination results can be undertaken only when S.B.A. are based on cognitive learning outcomes only or shown separately for scholastic and co-scholastic aspects but not when S.B.A. grades or marks are shown in terms of holistic assessment.

(ii) Whatever moderation is undertaken it must be in tune with the curriculum objectives reflected in terms of competency based teaching and testing.

(iii) Moderation of marking scheme may be taken up cooperatively by teachers and finalized through open discussion.

(iv) Selected examinees appointed in a specially organized meeting, may then be asked to mark the same scripts (5 to 10) and then the scheme can be validated further if the need be. This ensures well intended moderation of the developed scheme as also the assessment mode.

(f) *Intended Outcomes of the Moderation Process*

Since ultimate aim of moderation of assessment scheme is to make S.B.A. more acceptable, professionally tenable, administratively feasible and technically valid and reliable maximally, focal points in moderating S.B.A. is to make the teachers aware of the following action tasks:

(i) Unless quality of questions used for assessment is improved moderation is of no use.

(ii) Unless marking scheme is well developed in terms of intended process responses scoring objectivity in assessment will remain limited.

(iii) Unless subjectivity is assessing student is minimized by adopting different means suggested, public acceptability of S.B.A. will not be ensured to the desired extent.

(iv) Unless well organised training is provided to teachers-cum-examiners in S.B.A. we cannot expect our teachers for total objective assessment.

(v) Unless students are provided exemplar material and given some orientation for writing a good answer as per intended response they may not be able to appreciate between intended and observed responses.

(vi) Ultimate focus is on improving students' achievement and use not only validity and reliability of measurement.

14.4 How Best to Ensure Inter-school Comparability of Assessment Standards?

(a) Why ensure inter-school comparability of students, S.B.A.?

Since we have accepted that S.B.A. is necessary for wholistic assessment of pupils and know the role of teachers' subjective assessment, it is quite likely that teachers in different schools would use their own methodology of assessment and can use lenient or severe marking for assessing their students. Moreover, when S.B.A. marks are added or separately shown in Board examination certificate it may create unhealthy practices of boosting marks irrespective of actual attainment or performances. Therefore, for better compatibility of inter-school students' performance it is necessary to adopt such means or measures which become the basis of comparative study.

(b) Purpose therefore, is to ensure that by and large the different schools adopt the similar modes of assessment and ensure same quality of assessment vis-à-vis instrument of evaluation, thereby making it easier to compare students' performance on similar basis of assessment.

(c) Another purpose of comparability of assessment among different schools is to ensure that by and large validity and reliability of students' grading is ensured to the maximum extent. The more the difference in the validity and reliability of the measuring instruments used by different schools, the more difficult it would be to consider S.B.A. in different schools comparable. Therefore, purpose is to judge how far assessment devices used are equivalent to reflect on evidences collected, and used for grading.

(d) For better comparability of assessment among competing schools it would be necessary that modes of assessment used are the same. Besides scholastic tests, it would be necessary that co-scholastic aspects of testing are also broadly the same. It could better be in terms if well defined type of activities undertaken, projects used, and other co-curricular activities used for assessment of skills, attitudes, interests and other personality traits like cooperation intellectual honesty, etc. The same or similar activities used and co-scholastic aspects tested by different schools, the better it is for make inter-school S.B.A. comparable.

(e) In case of summative testing mode of assessment in term tests and annual tests it is desirable that after the tests are scored by the class teachers, the same set (one class) of scripts may be got assessed by another set of examiners picked up from the other school. This would not only provide evidence of the extent of objectivity in scoring as revealed by second set of scorers from institution other than the one whose students are being assessed on a summative test but it would also lead the teachers to minimize subjectivity in marking. This would ultimately result in developing marking schemes more carefully and lead to more reliable schemes of marking scripts.

(f) Validation of S.B.A. of different schools, in case of assessment of scholastic assessment against students' scores on board's examination results, would further provide evidence of a S.B.A. system with respect to cognitive development of learners. It would at least reflect well in the success of the S.B.A. system regarding curriculum transaction.

(g) Role of students can also be used to reflect on the usability of the scheme of SBA. Allowing students from different schools to comment on S.B.A. mode by teachers from different schools is also possible to reflect on impartiality of assessment on different scholastic aspects. If practicable, once in a year a full class comprising of about 5 students from different schools may be arranged and different teachers from different schools asked to evaluate the different aspects, both scholastic and co-scholastic aspects and final assessment marks awarded by each teacher on each aspect of assessment. This would provide good experience and evidence quality of assessment made by different teachers'.

(h) Involvement of different stake holders of reform in decision making process of assessment would also indirectly help in making S.B.A. a success. Therefore, role of students, parents, community, supervisors and counselors would help to streamline further the quality of S.B.A.

(i) A meeting of the representative principals of school be organized annually by the board in which decisions about the basic design of the S.B.A. system be discussed and finalised by involving different stake holders of reform.

(ii) Such a design should reflect the weightage to be given to various aspects of S.B.A. system both scholastic ad co-scholastic aspects.

(iii) It should also reflect time frame of various activities, tests and other assessment to help the teachers to undertake these as per schedule and guidelines provided.

(iv) This would help to develop a common pattern of assessment, reflecting attainment targettedness and minimize unwanted variation mode of assessment in different schools.

(v) At the level of Directorate of education and state institutes of education some case studies of S.B.A. may be undertaken annually and results circulated to schools to highlight adequacies and inadequacies observed in S.B.A. In case causes may be diagnosed and remedial measures suggested.

It is expected that above mentioned suggestions if properly followed then it will be possible to ensure comparability of school based assessment of students from different schools.

14.5 How Best to Combine Internal and External Assessment?

(a) *Why should we Combine Internal and External Assessment?*

(i) *To reflect total development or growth of the learners.* It does not need any evidence to support that any system of evaluation must certify total development of learner rather than reflecting his partial growth. The more comprehensive assessment is about learners the better it is for indicating his attainments in terms of both cognitive as well as non-cognitive learning outcomes ie evidences on total growth.

(ii) *To highlight teachers' credibility in assessing their students.* It is one concrete step to honour teachers' assessment and develop faith in their assessments. If teachers' assessments of their wards are not considered genuine for certification purpose, neither will the teachers be more careful in making assessment nor the students would bother about teacher based evaluation and respect their teachers for their grading and assessment.

(iii) *To reflect more comprehensive evidence in certification.* The more the evidences about various success indicators are reflected in the certification of students' achievement the more informative and reflective would be the certification of students' achievements failing which exclusion of teacher based assessment of non-scholastic aspects of development would remain neglected in teaching learning process. Focus on holistic development would not be practiced.

(b) *Bases of Combining Internal and External Assessment*

(i) *Decision about weightage to internal assessment:* To begin with weightage to SBA may be 20 per cent to 30 per cent as decided by the external agency (C.B.S.E.) conducting the external examination; of course in consultation with representatives of teachers, students, supervisors, principals, parents' associations and other stake holders. However, it may not be construed that this percentage is good enough to reflect teachers' assessment. After some trialling under strict conditions, it may be possible to make SBA more significant by raising it to 40 per cent or 50 per cent even. Idea is to give more and more importance to teachers' assessment and their right to assess their wards.

(ii) *Decision about weightage to testing and non-test techniques*: It has also to be decided so that besides the formative and summative tests like unit tests, term tests and annual tests importance in S.B.A. be also given to non-testing techniques of assessment like observation, inquiry and analysis which are usable for assessment of different co-scholastic aspects as required in other assessment activities, projects, games, social functions etc.

(iii) *Decision about Indirect versus direct grading*: Indirect grading via marking may be adopted in case of assessment of cognitive learning outcomes as in case of boards' examination but in case of assessment of attitudes, interests, personal social qualities etc. direct grading is desirable. Therefore, decision about weightage to testing and non-testing techniques has also be taken. Depending jupon the subject area 20 + 5 or 20 + 10 marks may be allotted for internal assessment of scholastic (20) and co-scholastic aspects (10) can be given to begin with. After trial for a year or two we may review the weightage keeping in view the experience gained.

(c) ***How to Combine and Reflect Assessment?***

(i) Depending upon the practice in boards' examination certificate marks or grades or both may be reflected in case of S.B.A. However, in the certificate indicate separately the grade of a student on internal assessment and external assessment, thereby showing that S.B.A. marks reflect on teachers' holistic assessment.

(ii) In addition, over all grade may also be reflected by combining grades on SBA and boards' overall grade which would provide basis for recording overall achievement level.

(iii) Another mode of combining may be to combine only SBA marks of students on summative tests only like term, semester or annual examination. This would ensure that in SBA a student's score on testing techniques combined with score on written examination conducted by the board, can better project students' total score on cognitive learning besides recognizing the SBA as authentic as external assessment, in which case this percentage of total marks on cognitive learning can also be shown.

(d) ***Modes of Certification of Students***

(i) There can be various modes of certification of SBA. In case of school certification grades can be reflected separately in case of assessment of scholastic and non-scholastic aspects of pupil development.

(ii) Total grading of S.B.A. by teachers may be reflected separately on the certificate issued by the board, along with board's grades.

(iii) Percentage provide further credibility to teachers' assessment combined percentage of score on SBA and boards' examination may be reflected.

(iv) Alternately, on the basis of research study and analysis of results, impacted by combining SBA with board's results, decision to reflect combined percentage in certification can be deferred till investigations show the extent of reliability of SBA of teachers.

(v) Whatever, mode of combining or reflecting SBA separately be adopted, certification of students should be as comprehensive and reflective of students' performance in terms of holistic development as possible in terms of subject-wise performance or success indicators considered desirable in prescribed curriculum.

14.6 How Best to Ensure Transparency, Autonomy and Accountability of Teachers?

(a) *Bringing Transparency in SBA*

(i) Purpose of each assessment should be made clear to the learner. In other words assessment objectives must be taken cognizance of by the class teacher. Is the oral testing to be done before teaching the topic in hand, to know whether students have already learnt the pre-requisite knowledge to understand the new concepts to be taught? Are students aware that class room questioning by teachers are used as a teaching device and not for assessment purpose? Do they know that questions given as home assignments are not for judgementing but for reinforcement of students' learning?

(ii) What is to be tested in terms of scholastic or co-scholastic aspects and content area to be covered in testing are to be clearly made known to examinees. What mode of testing to be used, oral or written or practical? Mode of testing is going to be a unit test, a single question or more, as well as form of questions, open ended, short answer or fixed response type like objective questions are pre-announced along with time frame.

(iii) Is it going to be individual based written test, or individual based activity test eg. a diagram to be drawn, slide to be identified or a school based assignment, etc. Is it going to be group testing? If yes, will it be an activity or a project each individual is going to undertake, as a group project or a quiz competition, providing prior information about weightage to each aspect of testing in terms of marks. This provides better transparency about the assessment mode.

(iv) Learners may be asked to check the marked script and if in doubt about the scores they get, they may be allowed to ask for review of marks whenever they doubt. This may help to rectify some discrepancy if any in marking and convince students of their inadequacies when review makes no difference in marking.

(v) In case of summative tests undertaken for grading, judgmenting or for promotion purposes, examinees if some of them are not satisfied, with their achievement scores and want to work more they may be allowed to reappear in the same test to improve their achievement, which indeed is the purpose of teacher based school assessments.

(b) ***Ensuring Autonomy of Teachers***

(i) Autonomy of teachers in respect of undertaking school based assessment should be ensured to the maximum extent since the teacher who teaches a class is the best judge to evaluate his students since he alone knows what has been taught and how the subject has been taught. Therefore, the principal of the school vis-à-vis Department of Education should provide full autonomy to a teacher than subjecting him to follow a given or prescribed pattern of school based assessment.

(ii) Teachers should have full autonomy to implement the scheme of SBA regarding what is to be tested, when to be tested and how best to be tested, grade his students and use assessment as a feedback device to improve students' achievement, of course following broad design of assessment introduced for S.B.A.

(iii) For particular mode of assessment in terms of assessment objectives, selection of particular assessment devices and tools of assessment, formatting of tests, time tabling, resetting question paper, using alternative activities and projects for assessment, re-examination of students on the same unit second time after remedial teaching etc. are all the privileges of the class teachers, having full autonomy of decisions.

(iv) He is free to involve students in testing by co-students or co-learners which makes the system of assessment learner friendly. Likewise, in various types of decisions about assessment system teachers are free to involve students and make SBA system a corporative venture.

(v) Teachers can get prepared their own question banks which they can use for assessment as well as for using as questioning device. Even on a giving topic or unit students can be asked to develop good questions based on various listed competencies to be tested. This provides good learning experience to students and for good instructions to teachers.

(c) *Ensure Accountability of Teachers for Students' Performance*

(i) Making teachers accountable for good system of SBA is not only necessary but essential to achieve intended assessment objectives. It is the teachers' responsibility not only for holistic development of learners but also for holistic assessment for which they have the responsibility of devising and practicing good system of school based assessment.

(ii) Accountability criteria may be worked out to make teachers serious, in order to minimize subjectivity in assessment and make the SBA more valid, reliable and usable which in turn make assessment more acceptable to public and professionally tenable.

(iii) In case of poor performance of students, poor assessment device, and tools of assessment used or other negative outcomes in terms of assessment objectives do reflect on teachers' accountability for which teacher has to be made accountable and need to be recommitted in the tasks of SBA.

(iv) Another way is to make teachers accountable for unsatisfactory results as reflected in board examination. Good or poor results do reflect on accountability of good assessment vis-à-vis teaching.

In fact accountability criteria for teachers has to be worked out cooperatively by the Department of Education with the help of subject-wise evaluation and curriculum experts.

Concluding Remarks

Historical perspective of Internal assessment practice, up to 19th century followed upto post independence, development in the field of examination reform, also provide evidences towards promoting S.B.A. Reflections in N.P.E. (1986) and P.O.A. (1992) about the role of S.B.A. is emphasised time and again as also reflected in N.C.E.R.T. Curriculum Framework (2009). Purpose underlying S.B.A. system is to make it an integral part of teaching learning process with emphasis on improving the measurement value of testing as well as on improving achievement of students. Different types of evaluation models are in use involving different process characteristics. Underlying philosophy of S.B.A. is the faith and conviction in teachers' competence and the credibility of their assessment. Concern for total development and holistic assessment of learners is the basic assumption leading to competency based, criterion referenced testing thereby making SBA a total school concept.

Intended objectives of S.B.A. is to establish more friendly learner system with a focus on pedagogical value of assessment to improve students' achievement, setting, maintaining and comparing inter-school performance standards. Key concepts underlying a good school based assessment system is to make it acceptable, credible, continuous, cooperative, comprehensive, improvement oriented, democratic, participative, objective centred and cost effective. International scenario reflects emphasis towards democratic, humanistic illuminative evaluation, ensuring inter-school comparatively of learners assessment and assessment of total school learning environment.

Conceptional map as well as model of S.B.A. is discussed along with operational strategy for effective implementation. How best to use S.B.A. to promote quality of education in terms of success indicators and applying quality control measures and providing research and other support services is the need of a good system of SBA. Undertaking institutional self-evaluation for improving learning environments of the school is considered significant to know as to where do we fail in implementing S.B.A. For successful implementation of a good scheme of S.B.A. we have to take cognizance of crucial emerging practical issues to make the scheme publically acceptable, pedagogically sound and functionally operative. And for that we have to ensure autonomy and accountability of the practicing teachers and bring transparency in the system of assessment.

References

1. Afzal, Ahmad (1993). *School Based Assessment Involving Students in Assessment Process*. West Sussex Institute of Higher Education.
2. Aggarwal, Y.P. (1998). *Statistical Methods: Concepts, Applications and Guidance,* Sterling, New Delhi
3. Ahmad, Youssuf (1993). *A Model for Using School Based Assessment,* Kenya National Examination Council.
4. Anastasi A. (1990). *Psychological Testing,* 6th edn. Macmillian Publishing Co. New York.
5. Berry (2005). Hongkong Institute of Learning. "Assessment as a catalyst to learning". Cheng Fung Ping (2002).
6. Best, J.W. and Kahan, J.V.(1986). *Research in Education,* 6th Indian reprint, Prentice Hall of India Pvt. Ltd., New Delhi
7. Bloom, B.S. (1956). *Taxonomy of Educational Objectives.* Handbook I. Cognitive Domain, David Mckay Co. Inc., New York.
8. Corey, S.M.(1953). *Action Research to Improve School Practices.* Teachers College, Columbia, New York, U.S.A.
9. Dadds, Hart and Susan, Marion (2001). *Doing Practitioner Research Differently,* Routledge, Falmer, London.
10. Dave, R.H.(1966/1969). *Taxonomy of Educational Objectives and Achievement Testing,* in Development of Educational Testing. Vol. I, London (In German and English) Munich.
11. Ebel. R. Frisbie, D.A. (2004). *Essentials of Educational Measurement,* 5th E.E.E Prentice Hall of India, New Delhi.
12. Garrett, H.E.(1973). *Statistics in Education and Psychology*. Vakils, Feffer and Simons. Bombay.
13. Gronlund, N.E.(1981). *Measurement and Evaluation in Teaching,* MacMillan, New York.
14. Hannah, L.S.A.(1975). *Comprehensive Framework for Instructional Objectives: A Guide to Systematic Planning and Evaluation*. Addison-Wesley Publishing Co., London.

15. Harper, A.E. (1990). *Preparing Objective Examinations,* Prentice Hall of India, Pvt. Ltd. New Delhi1.
16. Hill, P.W. (2005). *School Based Assessment: Why is it Important for Hong Kong.*
17. Hitchocock and Hughes (1989). *Research and the Teacher: A Qualitative Introduction to School Based Research.* Routledge, London.
18. Honery, Macintosh. *Use of Portfolio in School Based Assessment: Some Issues.* West Sussex Institute of Higher Education, England.
19. James, Mary (1998). *Using Assessment for School Improvement,* Heienmann Educational Publishers, Oxford, U.K.
20. Kliner, Paul, (1993). *The Handbook of Psychological Testing* Routledge, London.
21. Krathwhol, D.R. (1964). *Taxonomy of Educational Objectives,* Handbook II. Affective Domain David Mckay Co., Inc., New York.
22. Mauritius Examinations Syndicate (1994). *Proposed Blue Print of School-Based Assessment for Primary Stage in Mauritius.* Report of the 19th Annual IAEA Conference, Mauritius, 1993, pp. 277-286.
23. Ministry of Human Resource Development (1991). *Report of the Committee on Minimum Levels of Learning at Primary Stage.* Department of Education MHRD Government of India, New Delhi.
24. Morgan, Norah and Saxton Juliana (1991). *Teaching Questioning and Learning.* Routledge, London.
25. Mostyn, Coleman. *Ensuring Comparability of School Assessments Visitation and Moderation,* Senior Secondary Assessment Board of South Australia.
26. Naik, S.P. (2004). *Role of Evaluation in Education,* Anmol Publications, New Delhi.
27. Navodaya Vidyalaya Samiti (1989). *Scheme of Continuous Comprehensive Evaluation for Navodaya Vidyalayas,* MHRD Government of India, New Delhi.
28. N.C.E.R.T (2006). *Position Paper Focus Group on Examination Reform,* NCFW
29. Parlet and Hamilton, D. (1977). *Evaluation as Illumination: A New Approach.* (In): Hamilton, D. et al (Eds.) Beyond the Numbers Game. MacMillan.

30. Popham, W.J. (1978). *Criterion-Referenced Measurement*. Prentice Hall of India, New Delhi.
31. Saunders, N.M. (1967). *Classroom Questions. What kind?* Harper Row, New York.
32. Simpson, E.I. (1967) *Classification of Educational Objectives Handbook III,* Psychomotor Domain University of Illions, U.S.A.
33. Singh, Pritam (2009) *Dictionary of Curriculum and Evaluation.* Atlantic Publishers and Distributors (P) Ltd, New Delhi.
34. Singh, Amrik (2004). *The Challenge of Education.* ICFAI University Press. 52, Naearjuna Hills, Panjagutta, Hyderabad.
35. Singh, Pritam and Ved Prakash (1991). *Research in Educational Evaluation – A Trend Report* (In): Fourth Survey of Research in Education, N.C.E.R.T., New Delhi
36. Singh, Pritam (1978). Evaluation in Primary Schools – The Emerging Concept, *Journal of Indian Education.* Vol. IV, N.C.E.R.T., New Delhi.
37. Singh, Pritam (1978). *Taxonomy of Objectives and Paper Setting.* Punjab School Education Board, Journal, Chandigarh
38. Singh, Pritam (1993). *School-Based Assessment — The International Perspective.* Mauritius Examinations Bulletin No. 4, September, Issue, pp. 12-21, Special Issue on IAEA Conference.
39. Singh, Pritam (1984). *Performance Monitoring and Evaluation— A Framework and Operational Plan of Action,* UNESCO Consultancy Mission Report, Ministry of Education, Art and Culture, Mauritius.
40. Singh, Pritam (1994). *An Analysis of Operationalisation of Continuous and Comprehensive Evaluation Report of International Conference on School Based Assessment,* Punjab School Education Board, Chandigharh
41. Singh, Pritam (1994). *Setting Better Question Papers : The Scientific Way.* Bulletin 5, Mauritius Examination Syndicate, Mauritius.
42. Singh, Pritam (1996). *Toward Quality Questions,* New Age International Publishers Ltd., New Delhi
43. Singh, Pritam (2003). *Dynamics of a Question,* Doaba House, 1688, Nai Sarak, Delhi.
44. Singh, Pritam (2004). *Proposed blueprint of school based assessment. A Functional Approach.* Sahoday COBSE Newsletter Vol. No. LXIV.
45. Singh, Pritam (Ed.) (1986). *Evaluation at the Elementary Stage: A Book of Readings,* N.C.E.R.T., New Delhi-16

46. Singh, Pritam (Ed.) (1990). *Criterion-Referenced Measurement: Selected Readings,* N.C.E.R.T., New Delhi.
47. Singh, Pritam (1994). Advisor. Mauritius Examination Syndicate, Mauritius. Proposed Mauritian Blue Print of School Based Assessment for Primary stage.
48. Smith, D. (2005). *Measurement and Evaluation in Secondary Schools,* Common Wealth Publishers, New Delhi.
49. Srivastva, H.S. (1989). *Comprehensive Evaluation in Schools.* NCERT, New Delhi.
50. Stringer, E.T. (1996). *Action Research A Handbook for Practitioners.* Sage Publications, India Pvt. Ltd. B-1/1-1 Mohan Cooperative Industrial Area, Mathura Road, New Delhi-44
51. Thorndike, R.L. and Hagen, E (1970). *Measurement and Evaluation in Psychology and Education,* Wiley, New York.
52. Tom, Christie, *Improving Quality of Teacher Assessment Through Externally Designed and Internally Administered Performance Tests.* Centre for Formative Assessment Studies, School of Education, Manchester University. (1993 I.A.E.A. Conference)
53. UNESCO/UNICEF/World Bank (1990). *Report of the World Conference on Education for All-Meeting Basic Learning Needs. Jomtien, Thailand.*
54. Ved Prakash et.al (2001). *Grading in Schools N.C.E.R.T.,* New Delhi.
55. Wood, Robert (1991). *Assessment and Testing: A survey of Research.* Cambridge University Press, Cambridge, U.K.

Index